31 days of Christmas

31 Days of
Christmas

Roger Ellsworth

EVANGELICAL PRESS

EVANGELICAL PRESS
Faverdale North Industrial Estate, Darlington, DL3 0PH, England

Evangelical Press USA
P. O. Box 84, Auburn, MA 01501, USA

e-mail: sales@evangelical-press.org

web: www.evangelical-press.org

First published 1999

British Library Cataloguing in Publication Data available

ISBN 0 85234 436 8

Printed and bound in Great Britain by Creative Print & Design Wales, Ebbw Vale.

To new friends, good friends
Laura and Andrea

Acknowledgements

I am thankful to the Lord for the good saints of Immanuel Baptist Church, Benton, Illinois. These precious believers have for several Decembers joined me in contemplating with a sense of awe and wonder the truths of Christmas. I am also grateful to the editors and staff of Evangelical Press for their assistance in making this work possible. Special thanks go to my secretary, Laura Simmons, for her enthusiastic support and her many hours of devoted labour. Without her this work would not have been possible.

Contents

Introduction

As the apostle Paul contemplated God's glorious plan of salvation, he exclaimed: 'Thanks be to God for his indescribable gift!' (2 Cor. 9:15).

Christ is God's indescribable gift (John 3:16). He was given by an indescribably glorious person (God the Father) to an indescribably needy people (sinners) at an indescribably great cost (the hostility of sinners and the anguish of the cross) to bestow an indescribably great benefit (eternal life).

The Christmas season gives believers the opportunity to ponder anew this unfathomable gift. The meditations of this book are intended to lend a hand in that pondering. Ours is an age in which doctrine is disdained and Christmas is reduced to mere sentimentality. By rigorously focusing on Scripture's teachings about the gift of God's Son, Christians can avoid being swept along by the tides of the popular Christmas and be instrumental in, as the saying goes, 'putting Christ back into Christmas'.

Section I

Angels and Christmas

1.
The Christmas curiosity of the angels

1 Peter 1:3-12

There has always been a tremendous interest in Christmas, and now there seems to be an equal interest in angels. Angels are on television and in magazines. Angel sales are skyrocketing. Angel books continue to flood the market. Angel pins and angel figurines are constantly seen.

Polls indicate that most people believe in the existence of angels. One poll showed that 46% of Americans believe they have a guardian angel.

The Bible is also interested in angels, so much so that its authors mention them 273 times (108 in the Old Testament, and 165 in the New).

While there is a constant and ongoing interest in angels, that interest increases each Christmas. The Christmas season inevitably makes us think of angels. The angel Gabriel, as we shall see, was given the responsibility of announcing the forthcoming birth of John the Baptist, Christ's forerunner (Luke 1:11-20), to his father Zacharias, as well as the forthcoming birth of Jesus to his mother Mary (Luke 1:26-38).

A single angel announced the birth of Jesus to shepherds outside Bethlehem (Luke 2:8-12). No sooner were the words out of his mouth than he was joined by 'a multitude of the heavenly host' who burst into praise of God (Luke 2:13-14).

It is evident, then, that angels were closely associated with Christmas.

The angels' interest in salvation

The association of angels with Christmas runs far deeper, however, than merely announcing it. In our text, the apostle Peter asserts that the angels are intensely curious about the very matter Christmas was designed to deal with — that is, the salvation of sinners.

Simon Peter could not get over this business of salvation. To him it was the most marvellous and glorious thing imaginable. After addressing his readers (1 Peter 1:1-2), he immediately launches into a song of praise to God about salvation. He thanks God for the 'abundant mercy' that has given believers 'a living hope' (v. 3). He rejoices in the 'inheritance' that is 'reserved in heaven' for them (v. 4). And he freely and gladly acknowledges that all of this is made possible in and through the Lord Jesus Christ (vv. 3,7).

From this burst of praise for salvation, the apostle proceeds to make it clear to his readers that it fulfilled the prophecies of the Old Testament (vv. 11-12). This was only one of many evidences that the work of Christ was genuine and could be completely trusted.

Specifically, Peter asserts that the prophets of the Old Testament were enabled by 'the Spirit of Christ' to see both 'the sufferings of Christ and the glories that would follow' (v. 11).

Suddenly and unexpectedly Peter brings his discussion of this matter to a close by adding this phrase: 'things which angels desire to look into' (v. 12). The Greek word translated 'look into' is the same word used to describe what Peter himself did when he came to the tomb of the risen Christ. We are told that he stooped down and looked into the tomb (John

20:5). The same word is used of Mary Magdalene when she also looked into the tomb of Christ (John 20:11).

By using this word, then, Peter portrays the angels bending over, or, as it were, leaning over the balcony rail of heaven, to carefully and intently peer down upon the earth so they can see what God has done and is doing in and through the Lord Jesus Christ.

The Old Testament depicts the very same thing. On top of the ark of the covenant was the mercy-seat, where the blood of atonement was sprinkled by the high priest. And on each side of that mercy-seat was a golden cherub looking down at the very spot where the blood was sprinkled (Exod. 25:18-22).

Cherubim were also depicted on the veil that separated the Most Holy Place from the Holy Place of the tabernacle (Exod. 26:31). The Most Holy Place was that chamber into which the high priest entered once a year to sprinkle the blood on the mercy-seat. The depiction of the cherubim on that heavy veil also conveys the desire of the angels to look into salvation through the shedding of blood.

The reason for the angels' interest

But why are the angels so interested in the salvation of sinners? We are not surprised to read that the prophets of the Old Testament 'enquired and searched carefully' (1 Peter 1:10) regarding this matter of salvation. We can well understand them desiring to understand better those truths which they were prophesying. But what is this about the angels? Why do they marvel at the mercy of God?

We are out of our element here. Perhaps they study salvation out of amazement that God could love those who had so grievously sinned against him and were, therefore, deserving of nothing but his wrath. The book of Jude tells us that

there were also angels who fell into sin. These 'did not keep
their proper domain' because they rebelled against God, but
there was no salvation provided for them. They have rather
been 'reserved in everlasting chains under darkness for the
judgement of the great day...' (Jude 6; see also 2 Peter 2:4).
The fact that there was no salvation offered for the fallen angels must have made salvation for fallen men and women seem
even more amazing to the angels in heaven.

Perhaps the angels who have never fallen study salvation
out of amazement that the Prince of Glory, the eternal Son of
God, should stoop so low as to take unto himself the humanity of sinners, and in that humanity should suffer the hostility
of sinners and die on a Roman cross.

Perhaps they study salvation out of amazement at the peace
and joy of those who have received it. Could it be that there is
among the angels a bit of envy (sinless envy, of course) for
those of us who have been saved? Do the angels in heaven,
who have not sinned and never needed mercy, find themselves
wishing that they could experience the joy that such mercy
brings? The author of these lines seemed to think along these
lines:

> When I sing redemption's story,
> The angels will fold their wings;
> For angels never knew the joy
> That my salvation brings.

There is yet another reason why the angels are so keenly
interested in salvation. As we shall have occasion to note in a
later chapter (ch. 3), the angels are interested in anything that
brings glory to God, and nothing so glorifies God as his wonderful work of salvation. This work displays his grace, his justice and his wisdom in such a way that the angels, who delight
in his glory, cannot help but be fascinated by it.

In all likelihood the angels marvel at our salvation for all of these reasons and for reasons that have never even occurred to us.

The challenge of the angels' interest

It is all well and good to know that the angels are interested in salvation, but what does it have to do with us? The fact is that the interest of the angels in our redemption speaks a very powerful word to us.

The angels are God's mighty ones who 'excel in strength' (Ps. 103:20). The angels are God's immortal ones who are beyond the reach of death. The angels are God's faithful ones who ceaselessly and perfectly serve the God who made them (Heb. 1:7). And they stand in awe of redemption.

If God's mighty, immortal and faithful ones stand in awe of redemption, how much more should those who are weak, dying and sinful! If angels, who have never experienced salvation, are so keenly interested in it, how keen an interest should those have who have experienced it!

Is this the case? Is this characteristic of those of us who profess to know the Lord? Are we keenly interested in our Christ and the salvation he has provided? Is it evident to others that this is the most important thing in our lives? Is there among us a keen interest in learning more about our salvation? Do we enthusiastically seize opportunities to study the Word of God? Do we have a keen interest in expressing gratitude to God for our salvation? Are we anxious to join in public worship and sing praises to his name? Are we eager to do whatever we can to advance his kingdom?

Can we take the following words and truthfully say them to ourselves?

Pause, my soul! Adore and wonder!
Ask, 'Oh why such love to me?'
Grace has put me in the number
Of the Saviour's family;
Hallelujah!
Thanks, Eternal Love, to thee!

The author of the book of Hebrews saw the Christians to whom he wrote drifting away from the Lord and neglecting their salvation (Heb. 2:1-4). What would he say if he could observe us for a while? Would his assessment of us be the same as it was of those to whom he wrote? Would he accuse us of neglecting 'so great a salvation'? (Heb. 2:3).

It is such a great salvation that the angels of heaven themselves are intrigued by it. May God help us to see the greatness of it and to rejoice in it. Let's learn from the angels. Let's allow their interest in salvation to rebuke us for our lack of interest and to renew us in fervent desire to worship and serve the Lord.

2.

God's special Christmas angel: Gabriel

Daniel 9:20-27; Luke 1:5-20, 26-38

Christmas has to do with the salvation of sinners. Christ came to Bethlehem so that he could go to Calvary and there offer himself as a substitute for sinners. We have noticed that the angels are keenly interested in this matter of salvation. Since Christmas has to do with salvation, it is legitimate to say angels are interested in Christmas.

It is not enough, however, to say only that angels are acutely interested in salvation. Their association with Christmas goes much farther than that. Angels were also deeply involved in announcing Christmas. An angel appeared to Joseph to announce that Mary would bear a son who was to be named 'Jesus' because he would 'save his people from their sins' (Matt. 1:21). An angel appeared on the night Jesus was born to announce to shepherds the good news that a Saviour had been born (Luke 2:9-11).

No angel was more engaged in announcing the birth of Christ than Gabriel. The Bible records four appearances of Gabriel (two in Daniel and two in Luke), three of which dealt with Christmas.

The first of Gabriel's three Christmas appearances came almost five hundred years before Christmas became a reality. On this occasion he appeared to Daniel in Babylon (Dan. 9:20-27). Daniel had been reading his Scriptures to ascertain exactly when his people's period of captivity in Babylon would come to an end. Suddenly Gabriel appeared and announced that he had come to give him understanding (Dan. 9:2,22).

Daniel, of course, expected to be given understanding on the matter with which he was occupied, which was the end of his people's captivity. But Gabriel came to give him insight into a far greater matter, the coming of Christ. In effect Gabriel was sent to Daniel to lift his eyes off the pressing issue of the present (the date of Israel's release from captivity) to an event of far greater importance.

Gabriel's second Christmas appearance was to Zacharias (Luke 1:5-20). On this occasion he announced the forthcoming birth of John the Baptist, the forerunner of Christ.

Six months after appearing to Zacharias, Gabriel appeared to Mary to announce the forthcoming birth of the Saviour himself (Luke 1:26-38).

The close link between Gabriel's appearances and Christmas might well lead us to refer to him as 'God's Christmas angel'. On the other hand, the 'announcing' aspect of these occasions has led some to refer to him as 'God's preaching angel'.

The purpose of Christ's coming

As we examine the preaching of Gabriel on these occasions, we see certain major themes emerging.

First, we may say Gabriel preached the purpose of Christ's coming. In his message to Daniel, Gabriel said the Messiah would be 'cut off, but not for himself' (Dan. 9:26); that is, he would die, but his death would be for others. Through that death he would 'finish the transgression', 'make an end of sins', 'make reconciliation for iniquity', 'bring in everlasting righteousness', 'seal up vision and prophecy' (in other words, fulfil prophecy) and 'anoint the Most Holy' (Dan. 9:24).

There could be no better statement of the redeeming work of Christ. He died not for himself but for others, and in doing so provided forgiveness for their sins and eternal righteousness before God. After dying on the cross, the Lord Jesus entered into heaven to make intercession for his people and thus anointed 'the Most Holy'. All of this fulfilled not only the prophecies of Daniel but many other prophecies of the Old Testament as well.

The manner of Christ's coming

In his appearance to Mary, Gabriel stressed the manner of Christ's coming. Christ was to be born like no other. He was to be born of a virgin.

Gabriel explained it to Mary in these words: 'The Holy Spirit will come upon you, and the power of the Highest will overshadow you; therefore, also, that Holy One who is to be born will be called the Son of God' (Luke 1:35).

The virgin birth has been much disputed in recent years, but the evidence for it is inescapable. Two of the Gospel writers, Matthew and Luke, deal with it. Luke's account of the virgin birth is especially noteworthy because he was a physician and would have been naturally sceptical of a virgin birth. He begins his Gospel by telling us that he had examined carefully the entire gospel story. His words, 'having had perfect understanding of all things from the very first' (Luke 1:3), amount to his saying that he had 'traced all things accurately'. In other words, Luke's Gospel is the product of the painstaking research of a man not given to readily accepting myths and superstitions, and yet he is the evangelist who gives the fullest account of the virgin birth!

Herschel H. Hobbs writes, 'All of Luke's training and experience would deny the possibility of a virgin birth. To record such an occurrence as a fact would subject him to great criticism. Yet the evidence was so conclusive that he gave the most complete story of the virgin birth of Jesus on record.'[1]

Gabriel's message on the virgin birth emphasized an essential part of the gospel message. There could be no salvation for sinners without it. It is that important! The Second Person of the Trinity had to take our humanity in order to save us, but he also had to be different from us. If he had not been born of a virgin, he would have been exactly like us and could not, therefore, have done anything for us. In other words, he would have been a sinner himself and in need of redemption.

The duration of Christ's kingdom

In his appearance to Mary, Gabriel also stressed the duration of Christ's kingdom: 'And he will reign over the house of Jacob for ever, and of his kingdom there will be no end' (Luke 1:33).

Centuries earlier God had made this promise to King David of Israel: 'I will set up your seed after you, who will come from your body, and I will establish his kingdom... I will establish the throne of his kingdom for ever... And your house and your kingdom shall be established for ever before you. Your throne shall be established for ever' (2 Sam. 7:12,13,16).

That promise was now to be fulfilled. Jesus Christ is the King who reigns for ever, not over an earthly, political kingdom, but rather over a spiritual kingdom. This rule, now in the hearts of his people, will culminate in a kingdom of glory that will be universally acknowledged (Luke 17:21; John 18:36-37; Rom. 14:17; Phil. 2:9-11).

What a joy it is to be part of such a kingdom! When other kings and kingdoms have crumbled and passed away, the kingdom of our Lord will endure!

The necessity of belief

A final major emphasis in the preaching of Gabriel is the necessity of belief. This comes out very clearly and powerfully in his appearances to Zacharias and Mary.

Gabriel appeared to the former to announce that he and his wife would soon become the parents of a very special son, John the Baptist. He would play a unique role in God's plan by preparing the way for the Messiah (Luke 1:17). The birth of this special son meant the long-awaited Messiah was, as it were, standing right at the door!

But Zacharias and his wife were well advanced in years. They could not have a child! (Luke 1:18). The thing was impossible! So Zacharias gave way to unbelief and, as a result, was stricken with a severe judgement, namely, being unable to speak until after John the Baptist was born (Luke 1:20,22, 63-64).

While Zacharias refused to believe Gabriel's message, Mary quickly and readily embraced the message the angel brought to her although she faced an even greater obstacle to her faith. Zacharias had a historical precedent for the thing he was asked to believe. Abraham and Sarah had also been asked to believe that God would give them a son in their old age (Gen. 18:1-15). There was, however, no precedent for Mary. No virgin had ever conceived and given birth to a son.

Zacharias reminds us that it is possible to be an unbelieving believer — that is, to actually be a child of God and still refuse to believe the Word of God at one point or another. It is always tragic to see someone who believes in God and his Word fail to believe at a given point. It is much sadder to see someone never come to faith in God at all. The unbelieving believer robs himself of God's blessings, while the unbeliever robs himself of eternity in heaven with God.

How we need to take all of this to heart! So far as we know, Gabriel is not these days appearing to individuals to preach the glorious gospel of Jesus Christ. But that message is still being preached. And with the preaching of it comes the call to believe.

1. Herschel H. Hobbs, *Fundamentals of Our Faith,* Broadman Press, p.45.

3.
The Christmas joy
of the angels

Luke 2:8-14

We know the angels are capable of joy. The book of Job tells us they shouted for joy as they watched God perform his work of creation (Job 38:7).

The joy of the angels on that occasion must have been very great indeed. What fun to hear God speak a mere word and then see something pop into existence! Perhaps the angels exclaimed 'Ooh!' and 'Ah!' as they witnessed one act of creation after another. Perhaps we do not go too far astray if we imagine them conversing as they watched. A particular act of creation may very well have caused one to say, 'Wow! That was a good one!' Another act may have caused yet another to say, 'That's the one I like!'

How did the angels respond when they saw the first man, Adam, spring forth as a result of God's stooping down, taking a handful of dust and breathing into it? (Gen. 2:7). There must have been some 'Ooh's and 'Ah's then. This man, a little lower than themselves (Heb. 2:7), was God's special creature. He was made in the image of God (Gen. 1:26), crowned with glory and honour and set over all the works of God's hands (Heb. 2:7).

And what of the angels when man, that special creature of honour and glory, suddenly turned upon his Creator and sinned so grievously against him? (Gen. 3:1-7). Is it safe to say their joy turned to sorrow?

After the sin of Adam and Eve the Lord stationed cherubim at the entrance to the Garden of Eden. They, with their flaming sword, were to 'guard the way to the tree of life' (Gen. 3:24). Did those mighty heavenly beings look with sorrow and wonderment, first at the tree of life there in the garden, and then at Adam and Eve sadly walking away?

What was there about God's work of creation that would cause the angels to rejoice? What was there about man's rebellion that caused them to grieve? We know the angels are utterly devoted to God and to his glory. They therefore find inexpressible joy in anything that brings glory to God and sorrow in anything that robs God of his glory. They rejoiced over God's creative work, then, because it brought glory to God. It put his wisdom, his omnipotence, his sovereignty and his grace on display.

Conversely, they sorrowed over man's sin because the very essence of sin is falling short of the glory of God (Rom. 3:23). It is the creature thumbing his nose in the face of the Creator and saying, 'I will not have you ruling over me. I will be God myself.'

Evidence of angelic joy

If the angels of God so rejoiced over his creative work and so sorrowed over the marring by sin of that creative work, we should not be surprised to learn that they rejoiced at the birth of Christ.

In fact we may go so far as to say that their joy on that occasion far surpassed that which they experienced at creation. The greatness of their joy the night Jesus was born is abundantly evident. It is there in the words of the single angel, the herald, who announced the birth to the shepherds: 'Do not be afraid, for behold, I bring you good tidings of great joy

which will be to all people' (Luke 2:10). It is there in the anthem from the heavenly host that suddenly appeared to those
shepherds: 'Glory to God in the highest, and on earth peace,
goodwill toward men!' (v. 14).

The phrase 'heavenly host' would seem to suggest a great
number of angels were present. How many angels are there?
The psalmist says, 'The chariots of God are twenty thousand,
even thousands of thousands...' (Ps. 68:17). In the book of
Revelation, the apostle John says he saw 'ten thousand times
ten thousand, and thousands of thousands' of angels around
the throne of God (Rev. 5:11). We do not know how many of
those angels joined in the anthem that the shepherds heard,
but we may be sure it was an impressive number indeed.

The phrase 'heavenly host' may also suggest that every
kind of angel was present. Thomas Aquinas believed there
was a nine-level hierarchy of angels: seraphim, cherubim,
thrones, dominions, powers, virtues, principalities, archangels
and angels. We may doubt whether Aquinas was right, but we
do know that there are several different kinds of angels. And it
would not be surprising if the heavenly host in the skies above
Bethlehem consisted of some of each category of angels.

Reasons for angelic joy

It is not enough, however, merely to document the joy the
angels felt when Jesus was born. We must ask why they felt
this joy. What was there about the birth of Jesus that made this
such a joyous event for the very angels of heaven?

We have established that the angels of heaven rejoice when
God is glorified. Now we must say nothing has ever brought
more glory to God than this business of Christmas. Nothing
has so glorified him as his Son taking unto himself our humanity and in that humanity providing redemption for sinners.

How did the redeeming work of the Lord Jesus Christ bring glory to God?

The grace of God

We may answer by saying, in the first place, that the redeeming work of Christ glorified the grace of God. God would have been perfectly just if he had done nothing at all to redeem guilty sinners. He could merely have left all of us to the results of our sin, and no one could have accused him of being unfair.

But he was unwilling to do so. Instead he made a way for us to be forgiven and to be restored to fellowship with himself. That way was, and is, his Son, Jesus Christ. It was grace that compelled the Father to give the Son, and it was grace that compelled the Son to leave heaven and come to this dark world.

The justice of God

By his redeeming work the Lord Jesus also magnified, or glorified, the justice of God. It was not enough for the Son of God to come to this world. He could not have saved us by merely coming to this world. He had to do something specific while in this world. He had to satisfy the justice of God.

How few today realize this! God's justice had to be satisfied in order for us to be saved! There could never be salvation apart from this! From the very beginning, God decreed death as the penalty for sin — not just physical death, but also spiritual and eternal death.

That penalty had to be paid! If God had just set it aside, he would not have been true to his own word. God himself could not have let a single sinner go free without that penalty being paid. Here is the gloriously good news of the gospel: on the cross the Lord Jesus paid that penalty for guilty sinners. Yes, the Lord Jesus actually endured on that cross an eternity's worth of separation from God on behalf of sinners. There he cried out, 'My God, my God, why have you forsaken me?' (Matt. 27:46).

God was just to demand that the penalty for sin be paid once, but he would have been unjust to demand payment twice. If, therefore, Jesus paid the penalty for me, there is no penalty left for me to pay! Yes, by his death on the cross, the Lord Jesus magnified the justice of God.

The wisdom of God

Furthermore, we can say that the Lord Jesus Christ also magnified the wisdom of God. We might say the cross of Christ solved a tremendous difficulty — namely, how could God at one and the same time judge sin and let the sinner go free? Or we can put it in this way: how could God both satisfy his grace and his justice? His grace demanded that a way be found to forgive sinners. His justice demanded that sinners be punished eternally. God, in his infinite wisdom, found a way. Through the death of his Son on the cross, God satisfied both the demands of his grace and his justice. Justice saw the Lord Jesus Christ suffering in the place of sinners and was satisfied. Because Jesus took the penalty for believing sinners, there is no penalty left for them to pay and grace also is satisfied.

The redemptive work of Christ put the grace, the justice, the wisdom of God, and much more, on display and thus brought glory to God. And the angels, who rejoice when God is glorified, rejoiced in this work. They rejoiced when Jesus was born because that was the beginning of the work he came to do. As we have continually noted, the significance of Bethlehem lay in this: it led to Calvary. It was fitting, therefore, for the angels to rejoice above the fields of Bethlehem.

And it was fitting for the shepherds who heard the good news to rejoice as well. And rejoice they did! They went to Bethlehem, saw the child and returned to their flocks 'glorifying and praising God for all the things that they had heard and seen' (Luke 2:20). We do not need to have angels announce the good news of Christmas to follow the example of the shepherds. We can and must rejoice because the Saviour over whom the angels and shepherds rejoiced still lives and still saves. Now that is cause for joy!

4.
The Christmas sorrow of the angels

Hebrews 1:1-14

The angels of heaven rejoiced over the birth of the Lord Jesus Christ because it marked the beginning of his redeeming work in history, a work that was designed to bring glory to God. The angels always rejoice when God is glorified.

If it is legitimate to speak of the Christmas joy of angels, it would also seem to be legitimate to speak of the Christmas sorrow of angels. But what is there about Christmas that would cause the angels to be sorrowful?

The author of the book of Hebrews provides insight on this matter. He writes to Jews who had made a profession of faith in Christ but had begun to waver. Some of them had begun to wonder if they had been right to forsake Judaism and profess Christ. So this author takes up his pen and begins to write. He devotes more than half of his letter to demonstrating for his readers the superiority of Christ. He does this by showing how those persons and things most venerated by Judaism pale in comparison to Christ. Moses, the priesthood and the temple itself cannot begin to compare with the Lord Jesus.

The angels were among those most venerated by the Jews, so much so that the author begins his presentation of the superiority of Christ by showing how he far surpasses the very angels themselves. The author drives this point home by making note of what God has not said to the angels (v. 5) and then what he has said to them (v. 6).

What God has not said to the angels

What is it that God has not said to the angels? The author takes his readers to Psalm 2:7 for words that God the Father spoke to his Son: 'You are my Son, today I have begotten you.'

The Second Person of the Trinity is, and has always been, the eternal Son of God. John Gill correctly observes: 'Christ is the Son of God, not by creation, nor by adoption, nor by office, but by nature; he is the true, proper, natural, and eternal Son of God...'[1]

The verse quoted above cannot therefore mean that Jesus became the Son at the incarnation. It rather refers to the Father's declaring him to be what he had in fact always been, the Son. The Father made such a declaration at Jesus' baptism (Matt. 3:17) and on the Mount of Transfiguration (Matt. 17:5). But the Father issued his supreme declaration of Christ's sonship by raising him from the dead (Acts 13:33; Rom. 1:4).

God the Father has never made such a declaration to an angel. It is true that angels are referred to as sons of God in the book of Job (Job 38:7), but this is in a collective sense. God has never said to any single angel, 'You are my Son.' But he has said that to Jesus Christ, and the fact that he has said it shows the superiority of Christ.

Having established this, the author takes his readers to 2 Samuel 7:14 for additional words that God has spoken to the Son: 'I will be to him a Father, and he shall be to me a Son' (Heb. 1:5). These words, originally spoken to David, looked beyond David's immediate son, Solomon, to a far greater descendant, the Lord Jesus Christ. While Jesus was a physical descendant of David, he was much more than that. He was also God in human flesh, the Son of God.

What God has said to the angels

The author of Hebrews shows his readers what God has said to the angels by drawing a quotation from Deuteronomy 32:43: 'Let all the angels of God worship him' (Heb. 1:6).

The author says God spoke these words to the angels 'when he again brings the first-born into the world'. The word 'again' has caused some to think of the Second Coming of Christ. That would seem to be the time when God 'again' brings Jesus into this world. But since the previous verses deal with the incarnation, and since the angels obviously worshipped Jesus at that time (Luke 2:14), it is probably correct to translate the phrase: 'And again, when he brings the firstborn into the world...' In other words, the writer to the Hebrews is not using the word 'again' to refer to Christ's coming again, but rather to an additional argument for the point he is making — that is, the superiority of Christ over the angels.

His point is quite plain. Some of his readers were thinking about forsaking Christ and going back to Judaism, which venerated the angels, but they would be making a colossal mistake in doing so because the angels themselves worship Jesus!

What causes the angels to sorrow

With these things in place, we are finally able to identify the Christmas sorrow of the angels. It is the sorrow they feel when anyone gives to another the worship that belongs to the Lord Jesus alone. The angels worshipped him the night he came to this world, they worship him now and they will worship him with the redeemed (Rev. 5:11-12). And they are saddened when he is deprived of the worship he deserves.

This is, in fact, what is happening quite often. Worship that is to be directed to Christ is being directed to others. The angels themselves are, shockingly, being made objects of worship.

The Bible plainly forbids this. The angels are servants of God (Heb. 1:7), and God is to be worshipped. The apostle Paul writes to the Christians in Colosse, 'Let no one cheat you of your reward, taking delight in false humility and worship of angels, intruding into those things which he has not seen, vainly puffed up by his fleshly mind' (Col. 2:18).

Furthermore, the apostle John, as he penned the book of Revelation, twice received from angels the stern command that he was not to worship them.

John describes the first incident in this way: 'And I fell at his feet to worship him. But he said to me, "See that you do not do that! I am your fellow servant, and of your brethren who have the testimony of Jesus. Worship God! For the testimony of Jesus is the spirit of prophecy"' (Rev. 19:10).

The second incident is described in similar words: 'Now I, John, saw and heard these things. And when I heard and saw, I fell down to worship before the feet of the angel who showed me these things. Then he said to me, "See that you do not do that. For I am your fellow servant, and of your brethren the prophets, and of those who keep the words of this book. Worship God"' (Rev. 22:8-9).

In this age of angel-mania, we urgently need to remember John's experiences. Angels are not to be worshipped; God is. Angels are not to be offered prayer; God is. Angels are not to be praised; God is. Angels are not to be served; God is. The very angels this age so reveres are happiest when we are worshipping God, praying to God, praising God and serving God.

Why would anyone worship angels instead of the God who made the angels? A *Time* article offered this explanation: 'For those who choke too easily on God and his rules ... angels are the handy compromise, all fluff and meringue, kind, non-judgemental. They are available to everyone like aspirin.'[2] An article in *Christianity Today* says, 'Angels too easily provide a temptation for those who want a "fix" of spirituality without bothering with God himself.'[3]

We may prefer angels to God, but God has never allowed us to worship according to our personal preferences. Since he is the only proper object or focus of worship, it must be done the way he wants it done.

Furthermore, there is no salvation in angels. No angel has offered himself as a substitute for sinners, but Jesus Christ did. He alone is the Saviour. To ignore Christ, who holds in his hands the gift of salvation, and worship angels is akin to ignoring someone who holds a diamond in his hand in order to receive from another a worthless stone.

We are not completely out of danger if we merely refuse to worship angels. We must be very careful that we give no one the worship and honour that belong to Christ. There has been in the last few years an alarming tendency among evangelicals to bestow adulation upon Mary. All the angels of heaven understand that the triune God is to be worshipped. Mary herself understood that the Son she bore was to be the object of her worship (Acts 1:14). We most honour all the angels and Mary when we worship their God. We must worship God, and him alone, with all our heart, soul, mind and strength.

1. John Gill, *Exposition of the Old & New Testaments,* The Baptist Standard Bearer, vol. ix, p.376.
2. Cited by David Jeremiah, *Angels: The Host of Heaven,* Walk Thru the Bible Ministries, p.14.
3. As above.

Section II

A Christmas prophecy

5.
The littleness of Christmas

Micah 5:2; 1 Corinthians 1:18-31

Micah lived in dark, grim times. The people of his nation, Judah, were up to their ear lobes in iniquity. Obsession with money was everywhere. Disregard for justice was running up and down the land. True religion was dead and formal. The spiritual leaders of the nation were woefully deficient in morality.

While the condition of the nation may very well have been nothing more than a topic of conversation for the citizens in general, it was something far different for Micah. He was called to do something about it. He was called to boldly confront his people with their sins, to call them to heartfelt repentance and to assure them of crushing, devastating judgement if they refused to repent. To stand up openly while others sat, to speak while others maintained a polite silence, to arm himself with the truth of God while others melted into an easy, non-confrontational co-existence — that was Micah's calling.

Micah was equal to the task. Listen to him as he thunders: 'Zion shall be ploughed like a field, Jerusalem shall become heaps of ruins' (Micah 3:12). Judah was the tribe of David. Jerusalem was the city of David. David's descendant sat on the throne of Judah. And was calamity now to befall this nation? And was David's family to be cast away? Yes.

While it was often necessary for Micah to paint his messages with sombre black, that was not his only shade. He was

also able to lift up his eyes, look over centuries of time and see
a glorious future. He looks over at the little village of Bethlehem and addresses her:

> But you, Bethlehem Ephrathah,
> Though you are little among the thousands of Judah,
> Yet out of you shall come forth to me
> The one to be Ruler in Israel.

Bethlehem was to have a central role in the glorious future of
the people of God. Out of her the Messiah would come.

The reliability of God's Word

Certain truths emerge from Micah's prophecy that are worthy
of most careful study. For one thing, his prophecy had to be an
enormous consolation regarding the reliability of God's Word.

Bethlehem was the birthplace of David, and God had made
a covenant with David to the effect that his house would be
established for ever (2 Sam. 7:16). Micah's message about
judgement may have created something of a dilemma for some
of his contemporaries. How could such judgement be recon-
ciled with the promises that God had made regarding the future of the nation and the coming of the Messiah? Did the
looming judgement mean the destruction of the nation? Did it
mean that God's promise had been nullified?

Micah's word to Bethlehem, David's birthplace, had to come
as an encouragement to all who were vexed by this dilemma.
The Messiah, David's descendant, was going to spring from
Bethlehem and was going to rule in Israel just as God had
promised. God's Word was secure!

Centuries later, the Lord Jesus Christ was born at Bethlehem just as Micah had prophesied. We are wise if we let

Christmas remind us each year of all the fulfilled prophecies of Scripture, and if we conclude from those fulfilled prophecies that God's holy Word can always be trusted. And we are wise if we trust it — fully, gladly, implicitly, continuously.

God's delight in exalting the insignificant

There is more to this prophecy, however, than the reliability of the Word of God. Here we also get a glimpse into God's delight in taking something that is little and insignificant and exalting it.

It is noteworthy that Micah begins this prophecy by emphasizing the littleness of Bethlehem. Bethlehem was little in population, but it was not to be little in significance. Its name is as well known today as the great metropolitan centres of the world. Tokyo, London, New York, Hong Kong, Los Angeles, Bethlehem — no one would say that Bethlehem doesn't belong in that list of well-known places. But it doesn't belong there, as the others do, because of its great population, but rather because of what happened there. The birth of the Saviour made little Bethlehem well known for ever.

I have often wondered how modern men and women would have scripted Christmas had they been in charge. It would probably have been decided that the time of Jesus' birth should be delayed until the modern era of satellites and computers, and then his birth should be in one of the great media centres of the world. New York, London or Los Angeles would have done nicely. If the time of Jesus' birth could not be changed, it should at the very least have taken place in Jerusalem or Rome.

But God never does things as man would do them. He had no regard for the very things we consider to be important. He disregarded the big and flashy and glamorous, and his Son was born in tiny Bethlehem.

This was not some aberration on God's part. This is the type of action in which he delights. He not only chose Bethlehem to be the birthplace of his Son, but he also chose a mere peasant women to be his mother. And when the time came for Jesus to be delivered, it did not even take place in the finest facilities that Bethlehem had to offer, but rather in a crude stable. And the place where Mary laid him was not in a beautiful, ornamented cradle, but a manger. And the first people to come and pay homage to the Saviour were simple, rustic shepherds who had been out in the fields watching over their flocks.

It was no different in Jesus' childhood. He grew up, not in Jerusalem, but in Nazareth, a village so despised that there was a proverb about it: 'Can anything good come out of Nazareth?' (John 1:46). And his rearing in Nazareth was not in the grandest setting which that ordinary village had to offer, but rather in a humble carpenter's shop.

The humility of his birth and upbringing continued in the public ministry of Jesus. He spoke of the foxes having their dens and the birds their nests, but said that he, who was God in human flesh, had nowhere to lay his head (Matt. 8:20).

The apostle Paul loved to emphasize the humility of the Lord Jesus in coming to this earth. To the Corinthians he writes, 'For you know the grace of our Lord Jesus Christ, that though he was rich, yet for your sakes he became poor, that you through his poverty might become rich' (2 Cor. 8:9).

The truth is that the direction of Christmas for the Lord Jesus was all downwards: down from his glory; down to Bethlehem; down to the carpenter's shop in Nazareth; down into rejection in his public ministry; down into the depths of the fiery anguish of being forsaken by God on the cross; down into the grave. The only time Jesus went up is when the work the Father had sent him to do was all done. Then he ascended back into heaven's glory to take his place at the right hand of the Father.

Why is all this important? Why is it necessary for us to take note of God's pattern of stooping down to exalt the low and the humble?

The way of salvation

It is important for a couple of reasons. First, it tells us something of what is necessary for an individual to be saved. The way to salvation is down! It is to stop defending yourself against God and his Word and take your place in submission before him, owning him as your rightful Sovereign, and humbly accepting the salvation that he has provided in and through his Son.

As long as you are on your feet, spouting your opinions and making light of the shed blood of Calvary, you can be sure the grace of God that brings salvation is not working in your heart. When that grace works in a person's heart, it is with one grand purpose in mind, stated so aptly by the apostle Paul, 'that no flesh should glory in his presence' (1 Cor. 1:29).

God saves sinners by humbling them to the very dust so that the glory of salvation might belong to him, and him alone, so that all who glory will glory in the Lord (1 Cor. 1:31).

The key to blessing

It is also important for those of us who are Christians to be reminded of God's liking for things that are little and insignificant. This is the key to blessing for each and every child of God. If we want God's power to flow through us and to use us, we have to become little in our own eyes.

Paul reminds us of this in these powerful terms: 'Let this mind be in you which was also in Christ Jesus, who, being in the form of God, did not consider it robbery to be equal with God, but made himself of no reputation, taking the form of a bondservant, and coming in the likeness of men' (Phil. 2:5-7).

James and Peter also remind us of this truth in these forceful words: 'God resists the proud, but gives grace to the humble' (James 4:6; 1 Peter 5:5). James follows this word up by writing, 'Humble yourselves in the sight of the Lord, and he will lift you up' (James 4:10). Simon Peter follows it up by saying, 'Therefore humble yourselves under the mighty hand of God, that he may exalt you in due time' (1 Peter 5:6).

In these days of obsessive interest in self-image and self-esteem, we would do well to look again at tiny Bethlehem, and become tiny in our own sight.

6.
The largeness of Christmas

Micah 5:2; John 1:1-18

As we saw in the previous chapter, there is a littleness about Christmas. Our God delights in stooping. He delights in taking the little and the insignificant and making it significant. He took tiny little Bethlehem and made it the place of Jesus' birth.

This is more than just academic information that we are to salt away in our minds. It also contains a continuing principle for living. If we want to receive God's salvation, and if we want to be blessed and used by God, we must become little. If we are to find God and travel the road of his blessing we must become little and insignificant, like Bethlehem, in our minds and spirits.

But Christmas is not only about littleness. There is also a largeness about it. We see that largeness in Micah's prophecy to the village of Bethlehem. We find it right there in the words of Micah 5:2.

As we examine those words, we can conclude three things about the largeness of Christmas.

The largeness of eternity

The one to be born in Bethlehem was no ordinary baby. Far from it. He is described here as the one 'whose goings forth are from of old, from everlasting'. It is impossible to exhaust such a statement. Worlds of truth and meaning are enfolded in it. At the very minimum, we must note a couple of points.

The pre-existence of Christ

Our Lord Jesus did not begin to exist that night that he was born there in humanity. That was the night he took our humanity unto himself, but he existed long before that night.

How long has Christ existed? As long as God has. The apostle John writes, 'In the beginning was the Word, and the Word was with God, and the Word was God. He was in the beginning with God' (John 1:1-2).

Marvel, then, at the magnitude of Christmas. The Second Person of the Trinity, who was fully God himself and who was equal to God in every respect, stepped from heaven's glory and took unto himself our humanity. Who can fathom such a thing? It is beyond us.

The covenant made in eternity

The phrase we are considering also yields another truth, that of the covenant made in eternity between the three persons of the Trinity.

That phrase 'goings forth' relates, we are told by various commentators, to words that go forth from the mouth. Deuteronomy 8:3 tells us that we are to live on the basis of every word that 'proceeds' (goes forth) from 'the mouth of the Lord'. We must say, therefore, that the one who took our humanity there at Bethlehem, in addition to existing in eternity past, also spoke there.

Let's transport ourselves back through all the centuries of human history and beyond. Let's go back into eternity itself, to that time when there was not a single human being and not even the earth itself. Let's creep up now to the door of heaven and put an ear against it. God the Father is speaking about his plan to create the earth and to place man upon it. Man will be made in God's own image; that is, man will be a moral and spiritual being who will have the capacity to know God, love God and serve God.

As we continue to listen we learn that he is looking down the corridor of time and there he sees the man he proposes to create falling into sin. God points out that his justice will demand that the sinfulness of man be punished with eternal death. He also points out that, in his grace, he desires to find a way to forgive the sins of a host of men and women and restore these people to a relationship with himself. In saying this God raises the question of the ages: what can be done to satisfy both his justice and his grace? In other words, what could be done to punish the sinner and at the same time allow him to go free? How could God retain his justice and at the same time justify the sinner?

At that point there is a 'going forth' from the Second Person of the Trinity. He agrees to come to this earth as a man. Why as a man? The law of God requires that man should pay the penalty for sin. He pledges to perfectly obey the law of God in that humanity which he is to assume. Why? If he violated the law of God at any point in his humanity, he would have been guilty of sin himself and would not have been able to die for the sins of others. He further pledges to go to the cross and there receive the penalty of eternal death in that humanity, and by that death pay for the sins of all those who believe in him as Lord and Saviour. Thank God for that voice that went forth in heaven! There our salvation was planned!

Christmas celebrates the coming of the Lord Jesus Christ to do as he promised. What a tremendous thing it is! The eternal God himself came to this human realm as a man in order to carry out the word that he spoke in eternity past!

To measure the vastness, the importance, of Christmas, you have to be able to measure eternity itself. It is as large as eternity, and that is truly vast!

The largeness of Calvary

Micah's prophecy allows us to measure the largeness of Christmas in another way. On the basis of it, we can say the largeness of Christmas is the largeness of Calvary. Our peek into eternity has given us a glimpse of Calvary, but there is more that needs to be said about it. That more is found in the phrase, 'come forth to me'.

This is the Lord speaking through Micah to the little village of Bethlehem. He is foretelling the glorious future that awaits the people of God, a future in which Bethlehem was to play a central role. This future was to be made glorious by the coming of the Messiah and — note it well — the Messiah would, God says, 'come forth to me'.

What does this mean? It brings us to the very heart and core of the plan of salvation. We are in the habit of thinking of it solely in terms of Christ's doing something for us. But this phrase shows us that the plan of salvation also involved the Messiah doing something for God.

Do we understand this? God is the one who was offended by the sin of man. Our sin kindled his wrath, and before that sin could ever be forgiven that wrath had to be pacified. The only way it could be pacified was by spending itself. We were, of course, the deserving objects of that wrath but, as we have noted, God's grace compelled him to find a way for us to be delivered from that wrath.

What was God to do with his wrath, then? Here is the glory and the marvel of the Christian gospel! God spent his wrath against the sins of his people upon himself! God the Son took the wrath of God the Father in our place and our stead. That is why we find the apostle John referring to the death of Christ as a 'propitiation' (1 John 2:2). That word means God's wrath was appeased, or satisfied. Jesus did it by allowing God's wrath to spend itself on him.

The cross of Calvary is not just God trying to show how much he loves everybody. Yes, the love of God is there in its most powerful and forceful expression. But there is more to the cross than that. It was also the scene of a mighty transaction between God the Father and God the Son. It was God the Father expending his wrath and God the Son receiving his wrath — and all of it was done so we might go free. When you see the cross in those terms, you realize just how great the love of God was, and is, for his people.

A perfect picture of this truth is found in the Old Testament account of Abraham taking his son Isaac up the mount to offer him as a sacrifice to God. When Isaac enquired about what they would use for a sacrifice, Abraham responded by saying that God himself would provide the sacrifice (Gen. 22:8). And God did provide in that situation. He provided a substitute so Isaac could go free. But he also painted a picture of a future day in which he would provide for himself another substitute. This time the substitute was his own Son. God provided him for us in order that those who believe can go free.

This is how large Christmas is — it is as vast as Calvary's love. Who can measure that?

The largeness of royalty

Finally, Micah's prophecy allows us to say the largeness of Christmas is the largeness of royalty.

Why did God do it all? Why did he send his Son? Why did his Son take our humanity, and in that humanity do all that was necessary for our sins to be forgiven?

It certainly was not so that we could just shrug and walk away. God's purpose in giving his Son a people to redeem was so that his Son might rule and reign over those people. Micah's prophecy makes this clear. The one who was to be born in Bethlehem was to be born that he might be 'Ruler in Israel'.

Many took this to mean that Christ would set up an earthly kingdom, but his kingdom is not of this world (John 18:36). The Israel of God was never just national Israel. It was always those within the nation of Israel that embraced his plan of salvation. And Christ continues today to rule in the hearts of his people. Some glorious day that rule will be extended to the point where every knee will bend before him and every tongue will confess him as the only Lord.

Even to this day we consider royalty to be big and important. If royalty makes something big, then Christmas is big indeed because it celebrates the birth of the one who rules over his people and who will finally be recognized by all as, not just a king, but King of kings and Lord of lords.

7.
The tenderness of Christmas

Micah 5:4; Psalm 23:1-6

Micah's 'Christmas prophecy' certainly gives us much to marvel over. It seems to hold Christmas up as a jeweller would a diamond, turning it one way and then another in order to catch and enjoy the various aspects of it.

As we have seen, the second verse of this prophecy enables us to see and appreciate both the littleness and the largeness of Christmas. The littleness of it is that God stooped down to little Bethlehem to give his Son. God delights in exalting the lowly and insignificant. This is a part of the message of Christmas. The largeness of Christmas lies in the gift God gave. It was none other than his Son, the pre-existent, eternal Christ who came to offer himself as a sacrifice for sinners and set up his kingdom in their hearts.

The verse to which we now come enables us to see yet another dimension of Christmas, one which we sorely need. As we consider Christ coming from eternity to rule as King over the hearts of his people, we are likely to be intimidated. This new dimension to his coming allays our fears. It tells us that this sovereign Christ is a different kind of king. He rules, not as a tyrant, but as a caring, tender shepherd.

As we examine this verse, we can see various aspects of Christ's tender, shepherdly care.

The reasons for Christ's tender care

Let's first consider the reasons for this tender care. Two things must be said here.

Christ's ownership of the flock

First, Christ cares for his flock because of his ownership of them. They are, as Micah's prophecy clearly says, 'his flock'.

How did Christ come to have a flock? This brings us to the grand matter of redemption. Scripture tells us Christ has a flock of sheep because God the Father gave him one even before the world began.

It further tells us, however, that something else was necessary to make the flock completely his. His sheep were under the sentence of divine wrath because of sin. In order for Christ to make them his, that sentence had to be lifted. And the only way for it to be lifted was for the penalty to be paid.

So Christ came to this world as a man and went to Calvary's cross, and there he paid the sin debt on behalf of his sheep. He himself said, 'I am the good shepherd. The good shepherd gives his life for the sheep' (John 10:11).

There are those who would like to believe that all are part of Christ's sheep, that all that is necessary to belong to Christ is merely to be born into this world. It is unthinkable to them that a God of love would ever deny access to heaven to any of his creatures. Those who espouse this view limit the message of Christmas to these words: '… on earth peace, goodwill toward men!' (Luke 2:14). As far as they are concerned, those words settle the issue. The God who sent his Son into this world did so to express his goodwill, and his goodwill precludes any possibility that any will be eternally lost.

The problem with this view is that it focuses only on one aspect of the nature of God. Yes, he is a God of love, but he is also a God of holiness who is 'angry with the wicked every day' (Ps. 7:11).

The very existence of Christmas speaks to this matter of God's holy wrath against sin. If all are without exception headed for heaven, it was absolutely pointless for God to send his Son. But, if as Scripture emphatically affirms, men are by nature under the sentence of divine wrath, it was imperative for God to send his Son. Even the great 'love text' of the Bible, John 3:16, asserts that God gave his Son to keep men from 'perishing'. If there were no such reality as 'perishing', there would have been no reason for God to give his Son. God sent his Son to stand in the stead of sinners and to receive the penalty incurred by their sins so they would not have to perish but would have everlasting life.

Who is a greater authority on his flock than the Lord Jesus Christ himself? Hear, then, what he has to say about his sheep to the religious leaders of his day: 'But you do not believe, because you are not of my sheep... My sheep hear my voice, and I know them, and they follow me. And I give them eternal life, and they shall never perish; neither shall anyone snatch them out of my hand' (John 10:26-27).

Can words be clearer? There are some who are not Jesus' sheep. There are those who do not believe in him, do not hear his word and do not follow him. And their final destiny is to perish. Jesus himself referred to these, not as his sheep, but rather as 'goats', and spoke of a coming day in which they will be separated from his sheep (Matt. 25:33). On that day, they will hear from him these unspeakably sad and tragic words: 'Depart from me, you cursed, into the everlasting fire prepared for the devil and his angels' (Matt. 25:41).

Christ's sheep, on the other hand, are those who believe in him, hear his voice and follow him. These will not perish, but are safe for ever in the hand of Christ. On the same day in which the goats hear the sentence of eternal separation from

Christ, the sheep will hear these wonderful words: 'Come, you blessed of my Father, inherit the kingdom prepared for you from the foundation of the world...' (Matt. 25:34).

These are the objects of Christ's shepherdly care. They belong to him. They are his. Christ, as he points out in John 10, is not a hired hand who cares nothing about the sheep and who, therefore, quickly flees when danger arises. He owns the flock and cares deeply for each member of it.

The neediness of the flock

That brings us to a second reason for Christ's tender, shepherdly care, which is that his flock is made up of very needy sheep.

What basis do we have for saying this? As soon as Scripture uses the word 'sheep' to describe the people of God, it admits that they have great needs. Sheep are by nature very weak, needy animals. They have to be fed, watered, led, rested and protected.

Some sheep have special needs. Some are young and immature. Some are sick and feeble. Some have a tendency to stray. Some may even have to be encouraged to eat. Some are weary and may be prone to lag behind. Some fall into pits and ravines and have to be lifted out.

One doesn't have to be in the company of the people of Christ very long before one begins to realize that they are just as needy as sheep. Sheep are indeed a fitting emblem for those who belong to Christ!

As I look over my congregation each Sunday, I see many different types of sheep. I see some who are young and tender in the faith. I see some who are spiritually sick. They are not robust and strong in their faith. They are so ill spiritually that they are unable to keep up with the rest of the flock. Their church attendance is haphazard and spasmodic. I see some who are so lagging behind in spiritual things that they are in danger of falling prey to the predators who constantly follow the flock. I see some who have fallen into the pit of depression and the ravine of despondency. I see some who seem to have a constant tendency to stray. Is it not plain that Christ's sheep are very needy?

Christ's tender care for his people, then, arises from his ownership of them and from their great needs.

The nature of Christ's tender care

Micah's prophecy also enables us to see something of the nature of Christ's care for his people. Micah says, 'He shall stand and feed his flock.' The word 'stand' implies a couple of things.

First it carries the idea of alertness and readiness to act. What blessed consolation we have here! We needy sheep do not have a Christ who is lounging about in idleness. He is ever watching us. He is mindful of our needs. He is ever ready to step in and help us.

Standing also implies constancy. He is not moving here and there. He is firm. Here is another blessed consolation! The Christ who watches and cares today will be watching and caring tomorrow.

The word 'feed' may seem to relate to only one aspect of caring for the sheep, but that word should be translated 'shepherd'. What it means, then, is that Christ does for his sheep everything that any shepherd would do. That includes feeding, but it also includes providing rest and protection. It includes caring for those sheep with special needs.

A more complete picture of Christ's shepherdly care is given in the prophecy of Isaiah:

He will feed his flock like a shepherd;
He will gather the lambs with his arm,

And carry them in his bosom,
And gently lead those who are with young.

                                        (Isa. 40:11).

And, of course, another picture that is more complete is found in the 23rd Psalm. There the psalmist asserts the total sufficiency of the Lord's shepherdly care — even to the point where he is able to say, 'I shall not want.' That shepherdly care carries us all through life and extends even to the valley of the shadow of death (Ps. 23:4). Yes, the one who has so faithfully shepherded his people here can be counted on to shepherd them safely through death and into realms of glory.

Christ's care for his sheep can, then, be summarized in one word — sufficient. How we should rejoice in that sufficiency!

The basis of Christ's tender care

The final truth to be gleaned from Micah's prophecy about Christ's shepherdly care is the basis of it. How is it that Christ can provide such sufficient and tender care for his sheep?

The answer of the prophecy is that he is no mere man. He is a sufficient shepherd because he is clothed 'in the strength of the Lord' and 'the majesty of the name of the Lord'. In other words, his sufficiency flows from his divine nature and authority. He is nothing less than God himself.

As we look at the earthly ministry of Christ we can see him demonstrating the tender care of a shepherd. We see him opening blind eyes and deaf ears. We see him raising the dead. We see him forgiving sin. We see him proclaiming the truth of God. And as we look at all these things, we are made to realize that he had the signature of heaven upon him, and we are compelled to say with John the apostle that Christ is 'the only begotten of the Father, full of grace and truth' (John 1:14).

What a glorious Christ he is! And — awesome thought — this glorious Christ tenderly cares for and shepherds his people! What a blessed privilege it is to be shepherded by none other than the Lord of glory himself! May God help those of us who know the Lord to use this Christmas season to remind ourselves of this blessed truth — the baby born in Bethlehem came into this world with the tender heart of a shepherd. He manifested that heart all through his earthly ministry, and he continues to manifest it from heaven's glory towards all his people today.

8.

The happiness of Christmas

Micah 5:3-5; Romans 5:1-11

Micah's 'Christmas prophecy' has enabled us to appreciate some of the dimensions of Christmas. We have noticed the littleness of it, the largeness of it and the tenderness of it. Now we come to the happiness of Christmas.

First, I want to offer some words of clarification. By 'the happiness of Christmas', I am referring to the happiness produced by Christmas. And by 'Christmas' I am referring, not to all we have come to associate with that word (trees, lights, food, gifts), but rather to the birth of the Saviour there in Bethlehem. Now here is something that undoubtedly startles many — the coming of Christ to this world produces a genuine happiness.

Why is this such a startling assertion? It is startling because most of us do not think of happiness in terms of a baby being born in the village of Bethlehem two thousand years ago. Many would talk about a lot of things before that thought ever even crossed their minds: pleasures, sporting events, money, possessing the latest gadget, good health. All of these, and a thousand more, are generally considered to be the essential building blocks of a happy life.

Amazingly enough, many possess these things in abundance and are still fundamentally unhappy people. This indicates that it is time for us to rethink our assumptions about happiness and look towards that baby in Bethlehem once again!

Micah's prophecy enables us to understand how Christmas produces happiness. It first tells us what Christ produces. Then it tells us how Christ produces these things. Finally, it tells us for whom Christ produces these things.

What Christ produces

Micah uses two words to summarize what the coming Christ would produce.

Peace

One of these comes in the very last phrase of his prophecy — 'peace' (v. 5).

Everyone knows peace is part of the Christmas message. 'On earth peace, goodwill toward men!' was part of the praise the angels offered to God on the night Jesus was born (Luke 2:14). But we have a tendency to think of peace in terms of the absence of all conflict and, in particular, the absence of war.

Peace, however, is much broader than that. To have peace means to be at rest. It means we have tranquillity and serenity in every circumstance of life. It means we have an unruffled calm even in the midst of turmoil. It is to have strength under pressure.

Everyone is interested in having peace. We want to be able to handle all that life throws at us with calm assurance. We are so interested in it that we spend great sums of money trying to attain it. Counsellors, astrology, tranquillizers, psychiatrists — all are attempts to secure peace.

Micah's prophecy firmly declares that the peace we all so urgently want is found in none other than the Lord Jesus Christ. It is important that we understand exactly what Micah is saying. He is not simply saying that the coming Christ would *give*

peace. It is much stronger than that. He is saying that Christ
himself would *be* peace. Look at how he puts it: 'And this one
shall be peace.'

My peace is Christ! I can face life with tranquillity because
of him! When the storms of life assail me, I have in him one
who has promised to be my sufficient Shepherd. When friends
forsake me, I have in him one who has promised never to
leave me or forsake me. When I tremble at the prospect of
standing before God, I have in Christ the one who provided a
perfect salvation for all those who repent of their sins and
trust in him. When I step into death's chilly waters, I have in
Christ the one who has promised to meet me and escort me
into realms of glory.

No matter what the situation I am confronted with, I don't
have to pray for Christ to give me peace. I can look to him and
find the peace I need. He is my peace! And if I do not have
peace in any situation it is because I am failing to look towards and trust in my all-sufficient, unfailing Christ.

Permanence

The second word Micah uses to summarize what the coming
Christ would produce is 'abide' (v. 4).

This word carries a double significance. It can mean to sit
in undisturbed and unbroken peace. This is the result of what
we have been looking at — namely, having Christ as our peace.
But the word 'abide' also carries the idea of continuance. If
something abides it is not shifting or moving. It is not temporary or transitory. It is permanent and lasting.

We know all about impermanence. Houses crumble. Cars
fall apart. Marriages fail. Friendships disintegrate. Loved ones
die. And we ourselves die. We walk on this stage only for a
brief time, and then the curtain drops. Henry F. Lyte had it
right when he wrote, 'Change and decay in all around I see.'

How are we to respond to all this impermanence? Some just shrug and say, 'That's just the way it is.' They try to wring out of life every last drop of enjoyment before their own impermanence catches up with them.

But Scripture says impermanence is not all there is. The Christ who offers peace also offers permanence. The Gospel of John puts it in these words: 'For God so loved the world that he gave his only begotten Son, that whoever believes in him should not perish but have everlasting life' (John 3:16). Everlasting life is life that never diminishes, that never ends. It stays at the same level constantly and for ever.

We all want peace and permanence, and these things are found in Jesus Christ.

How Christ produces these things

How is it that Christ produces these things? The answer of Micah's prophecy is that 'He shall be great' (v. 4). There is no one like Christ. He is unrivalled and unique.

Great in his person

He is great in his person. He is the Second Person of the Trinity who is equal to God in every respect. When he came to this earth, he added to his deity our humanity, so that he who was fully God now became fully man — the God-man.

Great in his offices

He is great in his offices. We call him 'Christ', which means 'anointed one'. The Lord Jesus was anointed as Prophet, Priest and King. As Prophet, he proclaims the truth of God to us. As Priest, he made the perfect sacrifice for our sins so we can stand acceptably before God. As King, he rules over the hearts of his people.

There is no fault to be found in his discharge of any of these offices. We twist and distort the truth of God, but he never did. His sacrifice for sin was perfect in every respect. His kingly rule flows from a perfect love for his people and a perfect knowledge of their needs. When Jesus stood before Pilate the latter was compelled to say, 'I find no fault in him' (John 19:4).

I ask you now, what fault do you find in Christ? Point out one word which he mistakenly spoke. Point out one wrong deed. None can be found! He is what the disciples who were closest to him throughout his earthly ministry proclaimed him to be — 'without blemish and without spot' (1 Peter 1:19) and 'full of grace and truth' (John 1:14).

Now if this flawless, faultless Christ speaks to us about peace and permanence, we can trust him to be correct and accurate. If he says he can give these things to us, we can rely on him to do so. The greatness of his person and the greatness of his work preclude any possibility of his deceiving us on these vital matters.

Those for whom Christ produces these things

That brings us, finally, to consider those for whom Christ produces peace and permanence. Are these precious commodities the property of all without exception? Micah's prophecy emphatically says 'No!' Look carefully at verse 4. It begins with these words: 'And he shall stand and feed his flock...' And it ends with these words: 'And they shall abide, for now he shall be great to the ends of the earth...'

Do you see the connection? Who are the ones who abide? Those who are part of the flock of Christ! The peace and the permanence in this passage are predicated on being part of the flock of Christ. Those who are part of that flock are the ones who enjoy his tender care in this life and will continue to do so. They are the ones for whom Christ is peace.

So the most important and urgent question for each of us this Christmas is whether we belong to the flock of Christ. And that opens the door for another crucial question: how does one become part of the flock of Christ? There is no difficulty here. As we noted in the previous chapter, the Lord Jesus himself emphatically answered this question when he told the religious leaders of his day, 'But you do not believe, because you are not of my sheep... My sheep hear my voice, and I know them, and they follow me. And I give them eternal life, and they shall never perish; neither shall anyone snatch them out of my hand' (John 10:26-27).

Christ's sheep are those who believe in him. They have come to see that he, and he alone, can provide the peace and the permanence they need and desire, and they have turned from their sin and embraced him as their Lord and Saviour. They have heard his message of salvation and gladly accepted it, and now it is their intent and desire to follow him even as sheep follow their shepherd.

Section III

Christmas for the '-ful' family

9

Christmas for the fearful

Isaiah 7:1-14

We are all familiar with the '-ful' family. We spend a good bit of our time with them. Some of them are very appealing. Joyful, Prayerful, Hopeful and Faithful are among the most attractive. Other members of this family are unsavoury characters, to say the least. There are, to name just a few, Fearful, Sorrowful, Doubtful and Sinful.

Sadly enough, many of us spend more time with the repulsive members of the family than we do with the attractive members! They always seem to be knocking at our door and, all too often, we let them in. And they are guests that never want to go home!

I have good news for all those who have been hosting the unsavoury '-ful's. Among all the many benefits and blessings of Christmas, we can and must acknowledge this: it deals in a marvellous way with the dreadful members of the '-ful' family. It has the capacity to drive them from us and to bring peace and tranquillity in their stead.

The prophecy of Isaiah brings before us the sad spectacle of a man who was entertaining one of the '-ful' family. Here we have Ahaz, King of Judah, entertaining none other than that nasty and despicable character, Mr Fearful. Verse 2 of the passage we are considering says of Ahaz: 'So his heart and the heart of his people were moved as the trees of the woods are moved with the wind.' In other words, Ahaz and his people were frightened, terribly frightened. They were so afraid that their hearts were trembling within them.

The fear of Ahaz and Judah

What was the source of their fear? One of their neighbours, Assyria, was rapidly gaining strength as the major world power of the day. Kings of smaller nations viewed her expansion with great alarm and began forming alliances with each other. Pekah, King of Israel, and Rezin, King of Syria, had formed an alliance with each other, and they were putting pressure on Ahaz to join them.

Ahaz thought he knew a better way to stave off the Assyrian threat and thus secure the future of his kingdom. He decided to make an alliance with Assyria herself. That decision angered the kings of Israel and Syria so much that they decided to go to war against Judah.

As this chapter opens, Ahaz receives word of the advancing forces of Syria, and he is filled with a sense of dread and foreboding. What will happen to him and his people? How can they possibly hope to survive this threat?

Isaiah's cheering message

A gracious promise

While these and other questions churned and pounded in Ahaz's fevered brain, the Lord sent the prophet Isaiah to him with this cheering message of hope: 'Take heed, and be quiet; do not fear or be fainthearted for these two stubs of smoking firebrands, for the fierce anger of Rezin and Syria, and the son of Remaliah ... thus says the Lord GOD: "It shall not stand, nor shall it come to pass"' (vv. 4,7).

In other words, the Lord was telling Ahaz not to fear the kings of Israel and Syria and their armies. No matter what these enemies were plotting to do against Judah, the Lord had decided that their plans would not stand. Man's plans never stand when the Lord decides they should fall!

A gracious sign

After giving Ahaz this gracious word, the Lord proceeded to urge him to ask for a sign (v. 11). As a general rule, the Bible does not encourage us to ask God for signs, but this was the Lord's way of dealing with Ahaz on this specific occasion.

How the grace of God shines and sparkles in this account! The fact that the Lord ever speaks at all is sheer grace. The fact that he chose to speak to an evil king like Ahaz is an even greater manifestation of his grace. The fact that the Lord gave Ahaz the opportunity to ask for a sign is staggeringly gracious!

The Lord does not always express his grace in the same way, but he is always gracious. He is gracious to all in many ways, and he is gracious to his own in every way.

Ahaz responded to God's grace by stubbornly refusing to ask for a sign. He knew that if he asked for it, the Lord would give it, and he knew that if the Lord gave it, he would be obligated to heed God's Word. He had no place in his life for that.

But God was not to be put off. Ahaz was going to have a sign whether he wanted one or not. The sign was that a virgin would bear a son and before that child was old enough to know right from wrong, the threat posed by Israel and Syria would be completely eliminated.

There are many interpretations of this sign, but we can probably understand it in terms of an immediate 'natural' fulfilment during the time of Ahaz and a 'supernatural' (and greater) fulfilment in the miraculous birth of Christ. I believe that a young woman, who was a virgin *at the time* Isaiah gave this prophecy would, through the process of natural generation, bear a son and name him 'Immanuel' ('God with us') and that both Syria and Israel would be destroyed early in the life of this child. While I am not suggesting that this was a virgin birth, it may help us understand how Isaiah's prophecy had an immediate fulfilment: Syria and Israel were both destroyed just as Isaiah prophesied, the former in 732 B.C. and the latter in 722 B.C.

The second and larger fulfilment of Isaiah's prophecy came with the birth of the Lord Jesus. The first fulfilment required only that a young woman during the time of Ahaz should become pregnant and bear a son in the natural way. But Jesus Christ was truly born of a virgin. His mother was not only a virgin when she conceived him but also when she gave birth to him!

And while the child born during Ahaz's time signalled the presence of God with his people, the Lord Jesus Christ is in the fullest sense 'Immanuel'. He was nothing less than God in human flesh. Therefore, all during his earthly life, God was with people in a special way.

We might say, then, that God's way of treating Ahaz's fear was by pointing him beyond the dilemma that was vexing him to the glorious truth of Christmas. God treated his fear by calling him to look beyond his present circumstances to the coming Christ! It is almost as if the prophet said, 'Ahaz, the final cure for fear does not rest in the defeat of Israel and Syria, but in the coming of God's Son. This has been the hope of our people since our father Abraham, and you must make it your hope.'

Our fears

Ahaz was not the first or the last to have his heart tremble with fear. Many today have the same experience. Fear, like Satan himself, prowls about like a roaring lion, seeking whom it may devour. All kinds of fears haunt us: sickness, death, economic collapse, crime, environmental disaster and war.

On the other hand, multitudes are utterly oblivious to the one thing they should fear: an eternity without God. The Lord Jesus pointed to this sombre possibility in these words: 'But I will show you whom you should fear: Fear him who, after he has killed, has power to cast into hell; yes, I say to you, fear him!' (Luke 12:5).

Thank God, there is good news for all who find themselves in the clutches of fear. That good news is contained in the ancient words of Isaiah to Ahaz: 'Behold, the virgin shall conceive and bear a Son, and shall call his name Immanuel.'

We live on the other side of Christmas. Ahaz could only look forward to the fulfilment of these words. We can look back to Bethlehem's stable and see the fulfilment. There that night Immanuel was born. God took our humanity and took up residence among us and, in doing so, knocked a gaping hole in fear.

Child of God, what is your fear today? Bring it to Bethlehem and to the Immanuel born there. No matter how great it is, there is relief in that name, 'Immanuel'. God is with us! He is with us to sympathize with us. He is with us to help us. He is with us to guide and instruct us. We can face anything that fear dishes out if we know we have the eternal God with us.

But can we say Immanuel is truly with us? The Bible says he died, rose again and ascended to the Father in heaven. How can he then be with his people? Jesus answered this question in these words: 'The Spirit of truth, whom the world cannot receive, because it neither sees him nor knows him; but you know him, for he dwells with you and will be in you' (John 14:17). There it is! Immanuel is still with his people through the ministry of the Holy Spirit whom he sent into the world.

Now I want to say a word to those who do not know Jesus Christ as Lord and Saviour. I have already indicated that there is indeed something for you to fear, namely, eternity without God. I am happy to be able to say that you need fear this only if you reject the Lord Jesus Christ as your Lord and Saviour.

Why did the Lord Jesus leave the glories of heaven to come to this world? Why did he take our humanity unto himself? Why did he become Immanuel? It was all for the purpose of providing salvation from sin and eternal destruction. That salvation has indeed been provided, and now the good news goes out that this salvation can and will be ours if we will break with our sins and trust completely in the atoning death of Jesus Christ. Those who trust Christ for salvation have nothing to fear when they stand before God. Instead they can join the apostle Paul in these triumphant words: 'There is therefore now no condemnation to those who are in Christ Jesus...' (Rom. 8:1).

10.

Christmas for the doubtful

Isaiah 11:1-16

The prophet is here referring to the house of Jesse. It was a grand house indeed. It was from that house that the great King David had sprung. Jesse was his father.

It was while David was king that God made some staggeringly glorious promises regarding the house of Jesse. David was told that the promised Messiah would come from among his descendants, and that the Messiah would be a king like no other. While all other kings rule for a limited period of time, the Messiah would reign for ever (2 Sam. 7:16).

It would seem, in the light of these promises, that the house of Jesse was destined to go from victory to victory without so much as a single lull. It would seem that the lustre of the house of Jesse would never diminish.

The miserable condition of the house of Jesse

Now we travel rapidly forward to the time of Isaiah, and the future of the house of Jesse does not look so bright.

It was a terribly serious time. The powerful Assyrian Empire was running around gobbling up her neighbours, and the nations that had not been overrun were nervous and afraid.

Among these nervous nations was Judah. As her citizens surveyed the future, they found themselves wondering how long they could survive.

The survival of the nation was much more than a personal and political question. Bound up in it was this perplexing theological question: if the nation did not survive, what would become of all the glorious promises God had made to the house of Jesse? Specifically, what would become of that greatest of all the promises, the promise of the Messiah? The situation in Judah was so bleak at the time Isaiah was ministering that it appeared as if there would not even be a house of Jesse from which the Messiah could come. I can imagine a number of the people of that time saying something like this: 'Before the Messiah can get here the house of Jesse is going to be nothing more than a rotten stump.'

In the light of all this, we can say many in Judah were entertaining one of the more distasteful members of the '-ful' family — Doubtful. This doubtfulness, fuelled by the Assyrian crisis, was destined to become even more pronounced in the future. The Assyrian crisis was to pass, but a far more serious crisis would take its place, one that would see the Babylonians come into the land of Judah, destroy the city of Jerusalem and the temple, and deport the king and most of the citizens.

Those who had to endure the Babylonian ordeal would have even more reason to shake their heads in dismay over the house of Jesse. At that time it would look for all the world as if Jesse's house was nothing but a dead, decaying stump.

The message of the prophet

Into this fog of doubt and uncertainty strode the prophet Isaiah with a clear and cheering message. First, the prophet assured his people that the Assyrian threat would be only temporary

(10:24-25). Secondly, he declared that the Assyrian threat could not possibly make God forego or alter his promise to send the Messiah, nor, for that matter, could any other threat. God's promise was secure no matter how shaky it appeared to be.

The prophet firmly and triumphantly struck this note with these words: 'There shall come forth a Rod from the stem of Jesse, and a Branch shall grow out of his roots' (v. 1). The words 'Rod' and 'Branch,' according to Albert Barnes, refer to a twig or shoot 'such as starts up from the roots of a decayed tree...'[1]

The decayed tree was, of course, a reference to the house of Jesse. It looked as if it could not possibly survive, but as the prophet looked down the corridor of time, he was able to say to his countrymen, 'Don't worry about that dead, decaying stump. From one of its decaying roots there will spring a twig.' That twig was, of course, none other than the Messiah himself, the Lord Jesus Christ.

The fulfilment of Isaiah's prophecy

Let's speed forward again in time to the opening of Matthew's Gospel. The first thing Matthew does is take us through a genealogy. In the midst of this genealogy, he tells us, 'Jesse begot David the king' (Matt. 1:6). We knew that. But what about Jesse's house? Did it survive the terrible Assyrian crisis and the Babylonian Captivity?

The Jews of those times probably expected future genealogists to record: '... and the house of Jesse came to an end'. But as we read further in Matthew's genealogy we find no such statement. What we do find is this: 'And Jacob begot Joseph the husband of Mary, of whom was born Jesus who is called Christ' (Matt. 1:16). What looked to be a dead, dried-up stump in Isaiah's day was not so dead after all. From the decayed stump of Jesse's house the Lord Jesus Christ sprang up, just as Isaiah had prophesied.

Matthew gives us the genealogy of Joseph because Joseph, while not Jesus' biological father, was his legal father. Legally, then, Jesus descended from the house of David. But he also descended from it physically because his mother, Mary, was also from the house of David.

Luke's Gospel records for us the visit of the angel Gabriel to deliver this message to Mary: 'Do not be afraid, Mary, for you have found favour with God. And behold, you will conceive in your womb and bring forth a Son, and shall call his name Jesus. He will be great, and will be called the Son of the Highest; and the Lord God will give him the throne of his father David. And he will reign over the house of Jacob for ever, and of his kingdom there will be no end' (Luke 1:30-33).

Jesus, a physical descendant of David, was born to Mary, just as God had promised to David back there in 2 Samuel 7, and just as he promised to the people of Judah through Isaiah the prophet. The stump was not dead after all.

Perhaps someone will suggest that one part of the original prophecy to David has failed. That prophecy required not only that the Christ should spring from David's line but also that he should reign for ever, and Jesus, according to some, did not reign. This is true if we take his kingdom to be a temporal, political kingdom of this world. But the Lord Jesus himself insisted that his kingdom is not of this world (John 18:36), that it is in the hearts of his people (Luke 17:21).

The Lord Jesus Christ came to rule in and over his people, and there has never been a time in which that rule has not been in effect, and there never will be a time when it will cease. To the contrary, Scripture assures us that this inward reign is destined not only to become open but also to be universally acknowledged. The apostle Paul says a day is coming in which every knee will bow before him and every tongue will confess that he is Lord (Phil. 2:9-11).

Isaiah himself was enabled to see that day, and he rejoiced in it saying, 'For the earth shall be full of the knowledge of the Lord as the waters cover the sea' (Isa. 11:9).

The glory of it all

Why is it important for us to take note of the promises that were originally given to Jesse's house and the subsequent decline that made it look as if those promises could never be fulfilled? Why is it important for us to note that those promises were fulfilled and are still being fulfilled? The answer should be obvious. God has made promises to us as well. Our God is a promising God even to the point that his Word is fairly brimming with them.

One of the things that God has promised is that the same Lord Jesus who came there to Bethlehem centuries ago is coming again. And when he comes he will take his people home to himself into realms of eternal glory where there will be no more sorrow, no more crying, no more pain and no more death.

But, just as the Assyrians of Isaiah's day made it appear as if God's promise of a coming Messiah would not be fulfilled, so there are many 'Assyrians' today who make it seem as if the promise of eternal glory cannot be fulfilled. Who are these Assyrians? They are all those people, beliefs, lifestyles and circumstances that make the Word of God seem implausible and impossible.

The fact is, we live in an age of scepticism and doubt. Much of the Christian message is openly ridiculed. Christians try to stand firm against the doubt and scepticism of this day, but many find, before they know it, that Mr Doubtful has made his way into their house and pulled up his chair to their table. They want to have faith, but they seem to find themselves frequently entertaining doubt.

What are Christians to do when this is so often their situation? The answer is this: we are to look into the Word of God for those many instances in which God fulfilled his promises even when it seemed impossible for him to do so. And we are to deduce from those instances that our God can be trusted. It does not matter, then, how weak the cause of God appears to be in these days, or how many Assyrians there are to assure us that the promises of God are false. Our hope does not lie in how things appear, but rather in our faithful God.

I am always glad to see Christmas come round again for many reasons. One of the greatest of these is this — Christmas has a way of correcting our course. It has a way of driving the doubts from us and bringing us back to where we ought to be. It reminds us that God fulfilled his promise to the house of Jesse, and he will fulfil his promises to us as well. Christmas reminds us not to look at dead stumps, but rather to our living God.

1. Albert Barnes, *Notes on the Old Testament: Isaiah,* vol. i, Baker Book House, p.221.

11

Christmas for the sorrowful

Isaiah 9:1-7

There can be no question about the identity of the member of the '-ful' family being entertained here. Here we have the people of God entertaining none other than Sorrowful. The words 'gloom' and 'distressed' (Isa. 9:1) tell us as much.

What was the cause of this sorrow? The Assyrians had inflicted great distress on the northernmost tribes of Israel, Zebulun and Naphtali, and they were now hovering menacingly over the remaining portion of the kingdom of Israel and over the kingdom of Judah. So the people of Zebulun and Naphtali were already living in deep darkness (v. 2), and the dark storm clouds were gathering for many others.

It is possible that the words of the passage before us were sent by Isaiah to the distressed northern tribes to comfort them. On the other hand, Isaiah may have delivered this message to his own people, the people of Judah, to assure them of a glorious future that would include even those northern regions now under Assyrian control.

This much is beyond dispute: the message of Isaiah found its ultimate fulfilment in the Lord Jesus Christ. We know this because when Jesus began his ministry in the northernmost region of Israel, Matthew claimed it as a fulfilment of Isaiah's prophecy (Matt. 4:12-16).

We can say, therefore, that through the words of this pass-age the prophet Isaiah was comforting the sorrowful people of his day by pointing them ahead to the coming Christ. He was essentially saying, 'You must look beyond the sorrow of this time to the coming of the one who can drive sorrow away.'

We are also living in an age of sorrow. Millions know what it is to have the dark clouds of gloom hovering over them. Why are so many sorrowful today? 'Gloom-makers' abound. Sickness, death, financial hardship, family tensions — all of these, and many more, generate sorrow.

Sorrow is not, however, the only thing that connects us with Isaiah's distant day. Just as he pointed his sorrowing people to the Christ, so we can point the gloomy of our day to Christ. The only difference is that while Isaiah pointed to a coming Christ, we are able to point to the Christ who has come.

How does Christ drive sorrow away from human hearts? The prophet gives us the answer to that question by calling our attention to the four names by which the coming Christ would be known: Wonderful Counsellor, Mighty God, Ever-lasting Father and Prince of Peace. What balm and solace there is for the sorrowing in those four names! They affirm that each sorrowing child of God has four things in Christ that can drive sorrow away.

A wonderful counsellor to guide

First, we have a wonderful counsellor to guide us. When sor-row wraps us in its gloomy embrace, we feel the need for someone to come alongside us to comfort and guide us. And there are all kinds of counsellors who are eager to do so. The psychics tell us to call their hotline. The psychiatrist tells us to join his therapy group. Newspaper columnists tell us to write them a letter.

While there is an abundance of counsellors today, there is no counsellor like the Lord Jesus Christ. He is in a class by himself. When sorrow strolls down life's pathway and knocks at our door, he is there to understand and to offer sympathy and guidance.

Where do we find the guidance Christ offers? We find it right there in the Word of God, the Bible. The psalmist says as much. He knew what it was to have difficulty and sorrow, and in the midst of that sorrow he opened his Bible and began to read. And his testimony is that he found help and guidance there. He says to the Lord, 'Your word is a lamp to my feet and a light to my path' (Ps. 119:105).

The author of Proverbs also knew about the sorrows of life, and he knew what it was to find comfort and guidance in the Word of God. He says, 'For the commandment is a lamp, and the law a light' (Prov. 6:23).

If these men, the psalmist and the author of Proverbs, could walk with us through the sorrowful experiences of life they would say, 'Pick up your Bible and begin to read.'

What exactly do we find when we open our Bibles and begin to read? For one thing, we find that the sorrows of life are not meaningless and pointless, that our heavenly Father has our best interests at heart and is using our difficulties and sorrows to that end. We also discover that he is with us in the midst of those sorrows to strengthen and help us. And we are told that we shall find relief from our sorrows if we will come to the house of God for worship and to the throne of God in prayer.

But, wonderful as this counsel is, it will not help us if we do not read it and heed it. Those who do so invariably find the gloom of life dissipating and the light of hope and peace breaking through. What a cheering thing it is to have Christ's counsel to us through his Word!

A mighty warrior to defend

But there is more. When we are sorrowful, we also have a mighty warrior to deliver and defend us. Here we look at the term 'Mighty God'. That word 'mighty' is often used in Scripture in connection with warfare, and the people of God were accustomed to hearing their God described as a mighty warrior (Ps. 24:8; Zeph. 3:17).

The root of all our sorrows is sin. Yes, sin is the cause of it all. Do our hearts ache over sickness and death? Sin is the reason. Are our families torn with strife and dissension? Sin is the explanation. Are we gloomy over the condition of our nation? Sin is the cause. Take any problem you want, and you can finally trace it back to sin. All sorrow and gloom are rooted in the soil of sin.

If Christ is the one who drives sorrow away, he must of necessity be more powerful than sin. This title, 'Mighty God', assures us that he is.

Here is what we celebrate at Christmas: he who is God by nature took our humanity unto himself. Why did he do this? It was so he could go to Calvary's cross and die there. And why was it necessary for him to die on that cross? It was so he could deliver his people from their sin and all the sorrow that sin produces.

While the power of sin has in one sense been broken in the lives of those who have cast themselves on the redeeming work of Christ, there is in another sense more work to be done. Sin still clings to the people of God in this life, but, glorious thought, there is coming a day when our mighty God will destroy every last vestige of it. On that day, there will at last be 'no more death, nor sorrow, nor crying' (Rev. 21:4).

If you are sorrowful today, look to Christ, the mighty God, who alone has the power to defeat the thing that causes sorrow — that is, sin.

An everlasting Father to care

Thirdly, we have a Father to care everlastingly for us. It is an unspeakable blessing to know our Christ is the Wonderful Counsellor who has the wisdom to comfort and guide us. It is also a blessed thing to realize that he is the Mighty God, the warrior-king who has the power finally to remove all sorrow.

While we rejoice in these things, we have to admit that counsellors and warriors are not people to whom we feel especially close. There is always an element of detachment and distance there. But all that goes right out the window with the title 'Everlasting Father'. Here the prophet takes us to a much higher level, to the level of intimacy and closeness, by affirming that Christ is like a Father. In other words, he tenderly cares for us as a father cares for the needs of his children. He has a paternal, caring disposition.

Just as no caring earthly father can detect the sorrow of one of his children without being touched and moved by it, so Christ is touched and moved by our sorrow. And just as caring earthly fathers draw their sorrowing children to themselves for comfort, so Christ draws his people close to himself in many ways.

There are, however, enormous differences between the caring earthly father and Christ. The care of the former is brief and limited, but Christ's care is everlasting.

A peaceable prince to give peace

Finally, we have a peaceable prince to give us peace. The kings with whom the people of Judah were familiar seemed to delight in the bloody agonies of war, but the hallmark of the kingly reign of Christ is peace. He, and he alone, can cause us to be at peace with God and at peace with others.

But he also has the ability to instil peace within the hearts of his people. On the night before he was crucified, he said to his disciples, 'Peace I leave with you, my peace I give to you; not as the world gives do I give to you. Let not your heart be troubled, neither let it be afraid' (John 14:27).

No matter how severe his trials or profound his sorrow, the Christian can enjoy peace and tranquillity. He can do so because he knows that he has peace with God through the redeeming work of the Lord Jesus Christ, and even life's most ferocious storms can never change that. Further, the Christian knows that the peace he now enjoys with God will eventually usher him into an eternity in which no storms will ever rage again. Having peace with God creates peace within, and peace within has a marvellous way of softening the sorrows of life.

12.

Christmas for the sinful

Isaiah 12:1-6

Every year we hear countless statements as to what Christmas is 'all about'. Someone invariably says Christmas is 'all about' family, or sharing, or loving, or giving, or partying, and so on.

When was the last time you heard someone say Christmas is all about sin? No one ever says that, but that is exactly what Christmas is about. If there had been no sin, there would have been no need for Christ to come, and if Christ had not come, there would be no Christmas.

We have been looking at a book within a book. The prophecy of Isaiah contains what some scholars refer to as the 'Book of Immanuel'. This small book begins with Isaiah 7 and concludes with this twelfth chapter of the prophecy.

This is a chapter about deliverance. Some think it describes nothing more than the joy the people of Judah would feel when they were finally delivered from the threat of conquest by the Assyrians. While there can be no doubt that this hymn of praise was indeed a fitting response to that deliverance, we must go beyond it to the far greater deliverance that Christ came to provide. We have a scriptural precedent for doing this. The deliverance of the nation of Israel from Egypt, for instance, is used by the apostle Paul as a type, or picture, of the Christian's deliverance from sin (1 Cor. 5:7).

In addition to that we must remember we are in the 'Book of Immanuel', in which the prophet looks beyond the political situation of the day to that time when God would come to dwell among his people through his Son, Jesus. No mere political deliverance can begin to compare with the deliverance Jesus came to provide for his people.

Each Christian can, therefore, look back on his or her salvation and say to the Lord the very same things that the prophet here records. First, the Christian can truthfully say to the Lord, 'You were angry with me' (Isa. 12:1).

God's anger against sin

Nothing agitates folk more than for someone to suggest that God is capable of anger. An angry God makes them angry! As far as they are concerned, anger is beneath God and unworthy of him.

But nothing is more emphasized in Scripture than the wrath of God. The psalmist David writes, 'God is a just judge, and God is angry with the wicked every day ' (Ps. 7:11).

David was not alone in teaching this. John the Baptist gave prominence to it (Matt. 3:12), as did the author of Hebrews (Heb. 10:27; 12:25-29), James (James 5:9), and the apostles Peter (1 Peter 4:17-18; 2 Peter 2:4-9) and Paul (Rom. 1:18-19; 2:5; 3:5; 4:15; 12:19; Eph. 2:3; 5:6; 1 Thess. 1:9-10). The book of Revelation also stresses the theme of God's wrath (Rev. 6:16-17; 11:18; 14:10,19; 15:1,7; 16:1,19; 19:15; 20:11-15; 21:8; 22:11,15). And, most surprising to many these days, the Lord Jesus himself constantly warned about the wrath of God (Matt. 7:13-14; 22:13-14; 23:33; 25:30,41,46; Mark 9:42-49; Luke 16:19-31).

What is the cause of God's wrath? Our sin. Why is God angry with our sin? He is holy. No matter where we look in the Bible, we find God's holiness being stressed. Look here in the Old Testament, and you will find this prophet, Isaiah, having a vision in which the seraphim around God's throne cry, 'Holy, holy, holy' (Isa. 6:3). Look in the New Testament, and you will find four living creatures around the throne of God ceaselessly crying, 'Holy, holy, holy' (Rev. 4:8).

It is one thing to know God is holy, but quite another to know what that means. It means God takes sin with the utmost seriousness. He has a settled indignation against it and is set on judging it. It further means that God is absolutely committed to keeping all sin out of heaven. The apostle John writes of the heavenly city: 'There shall by no means enter it anything that defiles...' (Rev. 21:27).

These words caused one poet to write:

> There is a city bright;
> Closed are its gates to sin:
> Nought that defileth,
> Nought that defileth,
> Can ever enter in.

The Christian is one who has realized all this. He, just like everyone else, came into this world with a sinful nature (Eph. 2:1), but he, by the grace of God, came to understand something of the holy nature of God and how sin is an affront to him. The Christian is one who has also realized that he must some day stand before this holy God, and the thought of standing there in his sins overwhelmed him with despair.

God's anger turned away

But the Christian is also one who can speak of the anger of God in the past tense. He can say with Isaiah, 'You were angry with me' (Isa. 12:1). He no longer has to say, 'You are angry with me.' For the Christian the storm of God's wrath has subsided and died. It is past, and now he is able to say to the Lord, 'Your anger is turned away, and you comfort me' (v. 1).

What a gloriously wonderful testimony! Here is the picture. Here is the sinner in his sins and, because of that sin, the wrath of God is heading towards him. But before that wrath finally reaches him, something, or rather someone, steps in between the sinner and God and deflects that wrath.

We have a perfect picture of all this in the story of Noah and the ark. The people of Noah's day were also under the wrath of God. On that occasion God expressed his wrath by sending a flood upon the earth. That rain of God's wrath fell upon everyone except Noah and his family. It did not fall on them because they were in the ark God had told them to prepare. The rain fell on that ark but not on them. That ark came between them and the wrath of God.

Now let's stop to think about Christmas again. An angel of the Lord delivered this message to Joseph regarding what was about to happen to Mary: 'She will bring forth a son, and you shall call his name Jesus, for he will save his people from their sins' (Matt. 1:21).

An angel sounded that same theme on the night the Lord Jesus was born. To the shepherds outside Bethlehem he said, 'Do not be afraid, for behold, I bring you good tidings of great joy which will be to all people. For there is born to you this day in the city of David a Saviour, who is Christ the Lord' (Luke 2:10-11).

Christ came to save his people, the people given to him by the Father in eternity past, from sin! This is what these angelic announcements emphasized. And what did Christ do to actually provide salvation from sin? His taking our humanity by being born to Mary in Bethlehem, marvellous as it was, did not provide salvation. The importance of Bethlehem lies here: it was the first step on the earthly path that led Jesus to the cross. On that cross the Lord Jesus Christ did for sinners exactly the same thing that the ark did for Noah and his family. On that cross the wrath of God fell on Jesus, and since it fell on him there is no wrath left for all those who are in him.

The apostle John refers to this truth by calling Jesus 'the propitiation for our sins' (1 John 2:2). By using that word, John is telling us that Jesus appeased the wrath of God against sinners. He absorbed it in their stead. The great message of the Bible and of Christmas is this: God's wrath is either upon us or upon Christ. If God finds our sin upon us, he will send his wrath to fall upon us; but if he finds our sin upon Christ, his wrath against us will be turned away.

The Christian is in Christ and, therefore, can say the wrath of God has been 'turned away' from him. Because of that, the Christian can also use yet another phrase from Isaiah 12: 'O Lord, I will praise you' (v. 1).

The Christian's response

Consider again the central truths of the Bible. It tells us we are all in sin and justly under the condemnation of God, but it also tells us that this God has, in grace, provided a way for our sins to be forgiven. That way is his Son. Through him we are not only forgiven but are actually adopted into the family of God. As part of God's family we receive innumerable privileges and blessings in this life, and when this life is over, we have the promise that we shall be escorted into the incomprehensible and matchless glories of heaven.

In the light of all this, it would seem that it should never be necessary to urge those who know Christ to praise the Lord. But it is necessary. As we peruse the pages of Scripture we find the writers frequently urging the people of God to praise the Lord.

Prayer

What does it mean to praise him? Look at this twelfth chapter
of Isaiah again and note the emphasis on using the voice. We
are to use it in prayer. The speaker urges us to 'call upon his
name' (v. 4), which probably refers to praising God in prayer.

Proclamation

We are to praise the Lord by proclaiming his name to others.
We are to 'declare his deeds among the peoples' and to 'make
mention that his name is exalted' (v. 4).

Singing and shouting

We are to praise the Lord by singing (v. 5) and by crying out
and shouting (v. 6). The crying out and shouting refer to expressing joy by making a clear and loud sound. What better
way is there to do this than with a good solid 'Amen!' in the
public worship of the church?

Christmas reminds us that we have much reason to praise
God. A Saviour has come! We don't have to remain in our
sins and under God's wrath. We can be delivered. Those who
have received Christ have been delivered. This is what Christmas is 'all about'.

Section IV

The grace and glory of Christmas

13.

The predicament Christmas deals with

Romans 5:12-21

Would it surprise you if I said Christmas is the time when most people celebrate something they don't understand? Ask those around you what Christmas means, and you will find several explanations. Some will say it is the celebration of peace on earth and goodwill towards men. Some will say it is the celebration of family and friends.

Many realize such answers are not accurate when it comes to explaining Christmas, and they do not hesitate to assert that Christmas is the celebration of the birth of Christ. But even knowing that is no guarantee that a person really understands Christmas. Knowing that Christ came is a far cry from knowing why it was necessary for him to come.

Our celebration of Christmas will be greatly enhanced if we will take the time to delve deeply into its meaning. Let's begin with the beginning and God's marvellous creative work. The sun, moon and stars, the birds, fish and beasts of the field, the trees, grass and flowers — all were created by God.

The crowning piece of God's creative work was his creation of the first man, Adam, and his wife, Eve. The creation of Adam and Eve and their lives together in the Garden of Eden may sound like a simple story for the entertainment of children, but it involves the most profound truths imaginable, truths that Paul had in mind when he wrote the second half of this fifth chapter of Romans. The story of Adam and Eve in Genesis and the words of the apostle Paul can be compared to a fabric consisting of several threads, or a rope consisting of several strands. The threads or strands may, however, be separated and identified under the following headings.

A condition given

What was this condition? It is represented in Genesis by another tree, 'the tree of the knowledge of good and evil'. Adam and Eve were told not to eat of the fruit of that tree. All that was necessary for them to secure the blessing represented by the tree of life, then, was to comply with this one condition laid down by God. Perfect obedience to one command would have secured eternal life for them.

Why was it wrong for Adam and Eve to eat from this particular tree? It wasn't the tree itself that was evil. It was rather that this tree was what God chose to use as a test for them. He could have told them not to cross a certain river, or climb a certain mountain, or enter a certain cave, but he chose to tell them not to eat of the fruit of this one tree.

Why was such a test necessary? Adam and Eve were created with a free will, and a free will has to have a choice to make or it has no meaning or value.

A sentence pronounced

The next thread in this fabric is the sentence that was pronounced. God said that if Adam and Eve ate of the tree he had told them not to eat of, they would experience death. They would, in effect, forfeit the privilege of eating of the tree of life and would experience death in three forms —— physical, spiritual and eternal. Physical death is the separation of the soul from the body. Spiritual death is the separation of the soul from God. And eternal death is the separation of soul and body from God for ever.

Why would God pass such a severe sentence upon Adam and Eve for failing to live up to this one condition? Why didn't he just give them another chance? After they ate of the forbidden tree, why didn't God just say, 'We'll just pretend that didn't happen, and we'll try again and start from scratch'?

The answer is that God is perfectly holy and cannot ignore sin, or pretend it didn't happen. For God to do such a thing would be for him to compromise his own character and to deny himself and everything he stands for.

The blessing spurned

Now we come to the next stage, the stage in which Adam and Eve spurned the blessing of eternal life by eating of the tree of the knowledge of good and evil. Satan succeeded in getting Eve to eat by persuading her that she would become a god herself in so doing. Eve, in turn, persuaded Adam to eat also.

A principle revealed

That brings us to the next strand in this complex tapestry, which is the terrible tyranny of sin and death. At the very moment when Adam bit into that fruit, sin and death began to reign in his life. No, he and Eve didn't die physically at that very moment. That came much later. But they did die spiritually. The fellowship they had enjoyed with God was broken, and they hid from him, or at least they tried. God found them and drove them from the Garden of Eden and the tree of life.

A tyranny experienced

The final thread in this story is not found in the story in Genesis, but it is revealed clearly by the apostle Paul in his letter to the Romans — namely, the principle of representation that was at work in all of this. That means Adam was appointed by God as the representative head of the human race, and what he did on this matter of complying with the condition established by God and being entitled to eat of the tree of life did not count for him alone, but for every member of the human race. How furious some become at the mere mention of this doctrine! 'It's not fair that Adam should be allowed to act for the whole human race,' they cry.

But if we accept the Bible as the Word of God (and there is a mountain of evidence for doing so), we cannot escape this teaching that Adam was constituted by God as the representative of us all. I will not go any deeper into this matter of representation at this time, but I will only say that we should hold our tongues at this point because it is this same principle of representation that is our only hope for final salvation.

Because of this principle of representation, Adam's act of disobedience caused sin and death to begin their reign of tyranny over the whole human race. If you have trouble believing that we all fell when Adam fell, all you have to do is explain why we all die. Even babies die before they have the chance to commit a single sin of their own. Why? It's because sin and death are reigning in the human race.

Furthermore, if you have trouble believing we all fell with Adam you have to find some way to explain why we all sin. David says of himself, 'Behold, I was brought forth in iniquity, and in sin my mother conceived me' (Ps. 51:5). And what David says there of himself he says of others in another place: 'The wicked are estranged from the womb; they go astray as soon as they are born, speaking lies' (Ps. 58:3).

We can see sin in our own children. We do not have to teach them to lie, to cheat, to take God's name in vain, to lose their temper, to be selfish, or to show disrespect for authority. They simply begin doing these things and a host of others.

We can see sin in ourselves. Why do you find it so easy to lie, to think lustful thoughts and to take God's name in vain? Why do you have that desire to constantly run others through that shredder you call a tongue? Why do you practise being so difficult for your family to live with? Why do you find it so hard to do the good things God commands you to do, things like being faithful to attend his house?

We can see sin in our society. Murder and violence, sexual promiscuity and permissiveness, lying and stealing, child abuse, corruption in government, abortion, rape, shady business dealings, divorce, war, the creation of computer viruses and pornography are a few of the indications of man's sinful nature.

How much do we have to see before we admit something is radically wrong with man, and it is not just a second-rate environment or an inferior education? If a good environment is all that is necessary for people to be good, why are the things we see around us not restricted to the poor? If a good education is all that is necessary for people to be good, why are the evils all around us not restricted to the uneducated? Government officials are usually very educated indeed. Would anyone care to argue that they are free from evil?

Simple honesty compels us to admit that the Bible's message is being confirmed every single day. Our world is as it is because men and women come into it with a sinful nature, and that sinful nature is expressed in a thousand ways.

It is this problem of sin that Christmas was designed to deal with. The night Jesus Christ was born the angel announced to the shepherds: 'Do not be afraid, for behold, I bring you good tidings of great joy which will be to all people. For there is born to you this day in the city of David a Saviour, who is Christ the Lord' (Luke 2:10-11).

Why did Jesus come? He came because we need a Saviour. A Saviour from what? From this terrible tyranny the Bible calls sin. If it had not been for sin, there would have been no need for Jesus to come, and he would not have come. But because of our sin and because of his grace, he came among us. As one of us, he did everything necessary for our sins to be forgiven, and he now says to each and every one of us that if we want what he did to count for us, we must repent of our sins and trust solely in him as the only sufficient Saviour. Have you done this? Have you seen the depth of your sin and your helplessness to do anything about it? Have you seen that you have no hope apart from Jesus Christ? If not, I pray God will help you to see it today and to flee to the Christ of Christmas in true repentance and faith.

14.

The plan Christmas fulfilled

Romans 5:15-19; 1 Corinthians 15:45,47

The first man, Adam, was given the opportunity to secure eternal life for himself and for all his descendants by obeying God's command not to eat of the tree of the knowledge of good and evil. Adam failed to keep this command and unleashed upon himself and upon all of us the terrible tyranny of sin and death. We need do nothing but look around us to find abundant confirmation of the reign of sin in humanity.

God's standard, or requirement, for eternal life was perfect obedience, and Adam failed to live up to it and was driven from the Garden of Eden and the tree of life. If there was no more to the story of mankind than that, it would be a sad and pathetic story indeed and we would be the most miserable of all creatures. There is, however, much more.

Before Adam and Eve ever drew their first breath, God had a plan in place to restore to them what they were to lose through their disobedience. Adam and Eve were not programmed to sin, but God knew they would sin and he was not, therefore, caught off guard.

What was this plan God had in mind? The plan was a person! The Second Person of the Holy Trinity, the eternal Son of God, agreed with the other two persons of the Trinity, the Father and the Holy Spirit, that he would come into the human race as a second representative man, a second Adam and, as such, he would do what was necessary to redeem from Adam's fallen race all who would receive him as their Lord and Saviour.

What was necessary for him to serve in this capacity of a second Adam?

Christ's incarnation

First, he had to come into this world as a man. He had to come to this world because it was the arena, or realm, in which the first Adam had failed. But he could not just come to this world as God. He had to take unto himself humanity. He could not have been a representative head for men if he were not a man himself. He could not be another Adam apart from becoming man.

We are dealing here with the very heart of the Christmas message. The Second Person of the Trinity, who was fully God, stepped into human history as a mortal man. In doing so, he did not cease to be God because, as John Leadley Dagg explains, 'God cannot cease to be God.'[1]

He rather added to his deity our humanity, so that he was at one and the same time fully God and fully man without any contradiction or confusion between the two.

At Christmas we celebrate the coming of the eternal God among us as a man. We celebrate the truth of John's glorious statement: 'And the Word became flesh and dwelt among us, and we beheld his glory, the glory as of the only begotten of the Father, full of grace and truth' (John 1:14). We celebrate the glorious truth of Paul's simple statement: 'God was in Christ' (2 Cor. 5:19).

As marvellous and glorious as his coming was, it was not sufficient in and of itself to save us. Jesus did not come simply to be one of us, but to do what was necessary for us to have our sins forgiven.

Christ's sinless life

Therefore, the second thing he had to do as the second Adam was live a sinless life.

It was the purpose of Jesus in coming as the second Adam to undo what the first Adam did. The first Adam had failed to live up to God's standard of perfect obedience and, in so doing, had made it impossible for any of his descendants to meet God's standard of righteousness. We come into this world with a sinful human nature. Before we ever realize that God's standard for eternal life is perfect righteousness, we have already violated the laws of God in innumerable ways. Even after we learn about God's standard, we are not capable of living up to it. Our nature is such that we are opposed to God and to his demands, and as soon as we hear what God demands of us, our nature rebels and makes us want to do exactly the opposite.

Have you ever felt the weight of this dreadful dilemma? Here is a holy God who demands perfect righteousness of us, and here we are sinning with both hands!

This much ought to be clear to each and every one of us: if we are ever to meet God's standard of perfect righteousness, we are going to have to obtain that righteousness from someone else because we don't have any of our own.

Where can we get such righteousness? From the second Adam, Jesus Christ! He came to meet God's standard of perfect righteousness on our behalf. By becoming a man, he also came under the law of God. The apostle Paul stresses this aspect of Jesus' work in his letter to the Galatians: 'But when the fulness of the time had come, God sent forth his Son, born of a woman, born under the law, to redeem those who were under the law...' (Gal. 4:4-5).

As a man he came under the same responsibility that all men have, the responsibility to obey the law of God perfectly. We have all failed in that responsibility, but he didn't fail. The Bible bears testimony time after time to the fact that Jesus did not fail in this vital aspect of his work. Satan fiercely assailed him in the wilderness with three temptations, but Jesus didn't yield. He endured what the writer of the book of Hebrews calls 'the hostility of sinners', but he didn't allow such great provocation to lead him into sin. Jesus led a life of such pure, pristine moral beauty and excellence that even his enemies were compelled to admit they could find no fault in him (John 19:6). And his disciples, who from childhood up had been taught to believe no one is sinless, testified that he was indeed 'without blemish and without spot' (1 Peter 1:19).

The perfect life of Jesus usually receives scant attention. Most professing Christians will readily admit that Jesus lived a perfect life, but they seem not to have a clue as to why this was necessary. The answer is all tied up with Jesus' being the second Adam, the one who came to do what Adam failed to do. By his perfect life, the Lord Jesus Christ provided the righteousness that God demanded of the first Adam and still demands of us.

Christ's substitutionary death

That brings us to the third thing that was necessary for Christ to do in his capacity of the second Adam — namely, to die on the cross.

Jesus' coming to this world as a man identified him with us and qualified him to represent us, but it alone cannot save us. Even his perfect life is not enough to redeem us from the effects of Adam's fall. It satisfied God's demand for a perfect righteousness, but it did not deal with the sins we have already committed. Something had to be done to pay for those sins.

What was necessary to pay for those sins? The penalty of sin is death. God made that clear to Adam in the Garden of Eden when he said of the tree of the knowledge of good and evil, 'In the day that you eat of it you shall surely die' (Gen.

2:17). The Bible repeats this time after time. Ezekiel 18:4 says, 'The soul who sins shall die.' And Romans 6:23 tells us, 'The wages of sin is death.'

In order for Jesus to redeem his people, then, he had to pay for their sins by dying. Here we see again the importance of the first two points. Because Jesus lived a perfect life he had no sins of his own to die for, and because he was not just a man but was actually God in human flesh (and was, therefore, infinite), he could die for many people, not just one.

This is exactly what Jesus did on the cross. He had no sins of his own, but he took the sins of others on himself and paid the penalty for them. He died in the place of the sinners. The apostle Peter says Jesus 'bore our sins in his own body on the tree' (1 Peter 2:24). And Paul calls what Jesus did on the cross the 'propitiation' or 'satisfaction' for our sins. That means Jesus satisfied the wrath of God against sinners by actually receiving in his own body the penalty they deserved.

Jesus did, therefore, as the second Adam, everything that was necessary for Adam's sin to be reversed, and God tells us if we will stop excusing our sin, sincerely repent of it and cast ourselves completely on what Jesus has done, the perfect righteousness he provided with his life will be counted as though it were ours and the penalty he paid on the cross will be counted as though it were ours. With our sins paid for and the perfect righteousness of Christ covering us, we don't have to tremble before God's demands, but can go happily to heaven.

Those who receive what Christ did for sinners have the tyranny of sin and death broken in their lives. Spiritual death is replaced with spiritual life. The sentence of eternal death is removed, and the gift of eternal life is bestowed. And the sting of physical death is pulled so that it becomes nothing more than the entrance into eternal glory.

Those who receive what Christ did in his life and death find themselves joyously singing with the hymn-writer:

O loving wisdom of our God!
When all was sin and shame,
A second Adam to the fight
And to the rescue came.

O wisest love! That flesh and blood,
Which did in Adam fail,
Should strive afresh against the foe,
Should strive and should prevail.

Christmas celebrates Jesus in this capacity of the second
Adam. This was the plan of God for saving sinners, and Christmas is the fulfilment of the first stage of that plan. Have you
received this plan? Have you cast yourself in repentance and
faith on the work of Jesus as the second Adam?

Jesus is not only the second Adam; he is also the last Adam
(1 Cor. 15:45). That means there will never be another representative head of the human race. Each and every one of us
belongs either to the first Adam or to the second Adam. If we
belong to the first, we shall perish. If we belong to the second,
we shall live.

1. J. L. Dagg, *Manual of Theology,* Gano Books, p.205.

15.
The phenomenon Christmas celebrates

Hebrews 1:5-6; 10:5-7

We have been analysing the meaning of Christmas. We have noted the predicament that Christmas addresses and the plan it fulfils. The predicament Christmas addresses is sin. The first Adam failed to live up to God's standard of perfect obedience and unleashed upon the whole human race the tyranny of sin and death. The plan Christmas fulfils is that which the three persons of the Trinity agreed upon before the foundation of the world — that is, that the Son would step into human history as the second Adam and would do what was necessary to reverse the effects of Adam's fall for all those who believe in him.

It is essential that we understand these truths, but it is also essential that we feel something when we deal with these truths. In other words, it is essential that we be gripped by this phenomenon of Christmas. A phenomenon is something rare or unusual, something exceptional and out of the ordinary. It is something that causes us to pause and reflect, something that fills us with a sense of awe and wonder.

Christmas is the celebration of a phenomenon. It is the celebration of something of striking significance and awesome wonder, and it should not only challenge our thinking but also touch our hearts and shape our lives.

One of the greatest deficiencies of the modern church is that she has lost the sense of awe over these truths. We talk about the most glorious things the human tongue can ever express and we don't feel anything. We must be very careful that we don't do as many have done and just jettison our minds and seek nothing but feeling. We must have truth. We must apply our minds. But we must not be content just to assemble facts on the workbench of scholarship and leave them there.

This lack of awe is creating all kinds of havoc in the church. It stifles our worship and muffles our witness. It makes obedience to God a drudgery and yielding to temptation easy. It displeases the Lord and it delights the devil.

The author of the epistle to the Hebrews can help us to regain this sense of awe and wonder. In fact, his purpose in writing this epistle was to help Christians do just that. His readers were in dire need of recapturing the awe of their salvation. They were discouraged and despondent. Opposition and hardship had made some of them begin to think they should renounce their faith and go back to their former religion of Judaism.

What did this author have to say to his dull, drifting readers? Essentially this: 'Wake up! The Christ in whom you have placed your faith and trust is superior to all others, and Christianity is, therefore, exhilarating business.'

The words of the Son

In the process of shaking his readers from their sleepy lethargy, the writer to the Hebrews pulls the curtain back and gives us glimpses into the glory and wonder of Christmas. He tells us about that incredible moment in heaven when it was time for the Lord Jesus Christ to come into this world. What a moment it was! The Lord Jesus Christ stood up from his throne, and spoke to the Father these words:

Sacrifice and offering you did not desire,
But a body you have prepared for me...
Then I said, 'Behold, I have come —
In the volume of the book it is written of me —
To do your will, O God'

(Heb. 10:5,7).

What was he saying? He was at that moment taking the first step towards fulfilling the plan he and the Father had agreed upon from eternity past, the plan that required him to become a man so that he could provide redemption for men. The Father had prepared for him a human body, and he was now going to earth to inhabit it. In it he would be able to do everything necessary for sinners to be saved. He would, as we noted in the last chapter, perfectly obey God in that body, and would receive in it the penalty for our sins.

These words of Jesus to his Father at the moment of his incarnation refer to his perfect life and his substitutionary death. His intention to perfectly obey the Father in all things comes out in these words: 'Behold, I have come ... to do your will, O God.' And his intention to die on behalf of sinners comes out in the first phrase: 'Sacrifice and offering you did not desire, but a body you have prepared for me.'

The whole sacrificial system of the Old Testament was built around the concept of substitution. The offerer would come to the Lord with the realization that he himself deserved to die for his sins, but he would slay an animal instead. The animal became his substitute. The best such sacrifices could do, however, was to picture redemption. They could not actually provide it. The animals did not have a human nature, and could not, therefore, actually take the place of human beings. They certainly could not consent to being offered in the place of sinners. In taking the body God had prepared for him, Jesus was able to do what the animal sacrifices could never do.

The wonder of the angels

Imagine the amazement and wonder of the angels in heaven when they heard these words of the Son to the Father. See them as they travel with the Son to the outskirts of heaven and then watch in wonderment as he becomes, not a full-grown man (which would have been amazing enough), but a tiny baby. He who was God was now clothed in human flesh.

The Bible says the angels long to look into the things of God (1 Peter 1:12), and we may rest assured they carefully observed each stage of God's redemptive plan and puzzled over the meaning of it all.

They had seen it all. They were there when God the Father spoke all the worlds into existence, and the Bible tells us that they shouted for joy over the marvel of creation (Job 38:7).

They were there when Adam fell and introduced the terrible ravages of sin into the human race. They must have wondered how Adam could be so ungrateful to the God who had made him and blessed him as to disobey the one commandment given him by the Lord.

They were there when God announced to Adam and Eve that he had a plan to reverse the effects of Adam's fall, a plan to redeem from the terrible effects of sin. They heard the promise that this redemption would be made available through the seed of the woman, and that the bruising of his heel would lead to the crushing of the serpent's head (Gen. 3:15).

They were there when God first pictured redemption through the death of a substitute by killing animals and making coats of skins for Adam and Eve.

They were there when God told each household in Israel to kill a lamb and smear its blood on their doorposts, and one of them was assigned the task of carrying out God's death sentence on all the first-born who were not in a house marked with blood.

They were there when God instituted the sacrificial system in the nation of Israel.

How much did they understand? We cannot say with certainty. They must have known the Lord Jesus was going to come into human history, but the author of Hebrews implies that there was some uncertainty on their part as to how they were now to respond to this amazing fact of their God being clothed in human flesh. We gather this from what God the Father said to them: 'Let all the angels of God worship him' (Heb. 1:6). Yes, the Second Person of the Trinity was now in human flesh, but he was no less God than he had been before, and he was, therefore, still to be the object of their worship and praise.

The angels did not have to wait long to worship their God now clothed in human flesh. One of them was first to announce this new thing that God had done to some shepherds: 'Do not be afraid, for behold, I bring you good tidings of great joy which will be to all people. For there is born to you this day in the city of David a Saviour, who is Christ the Lord' (Luke 2:10-11). And then a whole multitude of them were given their first opportunity to obey God's new commandment and worship this glorious person who was now God in human flesh. Luke says, 'And suddenly there was with the angel a multitude of the heavenly host praising God and saying: "Glory to God in the highest, and on earth peace, good will toward men!"' (Luke 2:13-14).

The angels of heaven stood in awe of what God did at Christmas, and they were primarily mere spectators or bystanders. They were not involved in Christmas to the degree that we are. How are we involved? He came for us! His coming was observed by angels, but it was designed for sinful human beings. That which amazed and awed heaven's angels was undertaken with us in mind and for our eternal benefit and welfare.

It was undertaken so that we might be freed from the tyranny of sin and death and might be given everlasting life. God the Son took a human body so that he might in that body render perfect obedience to God and receive in that body the penalty we deserve for our sins. God the Son took a human body so what he did in that body might be imputed, or counted, for all those who will forsake their sins and cast themselves completely upon him.

It was for us he came and it was for us he died. The apostle Paul puts it in these terms: 'For you know the grace of our Lord Jesus Christ, that though he was rich, yet for your sakes he became poor, that you through his poverty might become rich' (2 Cor. 8:9).

Oh, what a chasm he crossed — from heaven to earth; from heaven's glorious throne to Bethlehem's crude stable and manger; from riches to poverty; from angels' praises to the hostility of sinners; from a perfect environment to a world of sin and shame! And it was all for his people.

If the angels, who were not the beneficiaries of Christ's coming, stood in awe of it all, how much more should we! If the angels worshipped their God in human flesh, how much more should we!

16.

The pattern Christmas sets

Philippians 2:1-11

Christmas is God's plan for dealing with the terrible predicament of our sin, and it is such a glorious and wonderful plan that we should stand in awe of it. God's people rejoice in these wondrous truths each Christmas season, and it is right and proper that we should do so. But if we are not careful we can fall into the trap of restricting or confining the truths of Christmas to one particular time of year.

In these much-loved verses, the apostle Paul shows us a principle at work in Christ's coming that is to be at work in the lives of all God's people each and every day. In other words, when the Second Person of the Trinity stepped into human history as a man he set a pattern, or example, for his people to follow.

It should go without saying that we cannot perfectly imitate this pattern that Christ set. There are dimensions to Christ's incarnation that are unique and unrepeatable, but we can act in accordance with the same principle, the same spirit or disposition that was at work in Jesus Christ when he took unto himself our humanity.

Let's examine this passage to see what we can learn about the pattern that Christ sets for children of God.

There are three aspects about this pattern that demand our attention.

A clear pattern

First, it is a very clear pattern. What pattern did Jesus set for us when he came to this earth? What principle activated him? It was the pattern, or principle, of selflessness.

Stop and think about it. The Lord Jesus Christ existed in eternal glory with the Father before he ever came to this world. He not only existed with God, but he was God himself. He was honoured by the angels as God. He exercised all the prerogatives of God, and enjoyed all the glories of heaven.

The Lord Jesus could have clung to these things. He did not have to agree to take our humanity. He did not have to come to this dark world. He could rightly have said, 'Those people don't deserve to be saved from their sins.' He could have insisted on his rights and no one could have faulted him. But he didn't. He did not cling to his divine prerogatives. He did not consider all the glories of heaven and all the trappings of deity as things that must be clung to and protected at all costs. Instead he laid them all aside. No, he did not cease to be God when he took on humanity, but he did strip himself of all the trappings of glory.

He would have stooped low had he become a rich man born into a powerful, prestigious family, but he stooped so low that he actually took 'the form of a bondservant' (v. 7). He would have stooped low if he had become a man who lived an ordinary life and died an ordinary death, but he stooped so low that his life was that of a bondservant and his death was one in which he experienced the bitter agony of being forsaken by God.

Selflessness was the spirit that motivated him, and his lowly birth, his servant life and his sacrificial death were the manifestations of that principle of selflessness.

Do you realize what this means? It means that if we follow the pattern established by Christ in his coming we cannot live for ourselves, but we must live for others. It means we cannot insist on our own rights, but must seek the good of others. It means we must wear our possessions loosely and be ready to make sacrifices for the good of others.

How important is that word 'others' to us? Does it rank anywhere near the top of our list of priorities? Or has it been pushed to the bottom by words like 'I', 'me', 'mine' and 'my'?

It has been reported that General William Booth, the founder of the Salvation Army, was invited to give an address to a convention but fell ill and was unable to attend. When it was announced that he had sent a telegram, those attending the conference expected a very moving and profound statement from the grand old saint, but his message consisted of one word — 'Others'.[1]

That word forces those of us who are Christians to think in terms of two categories: those who are not Christians and those who are. Imitating the pattern of Christ regarding those in the first category means we must be willing to renounce comfort and rights and be willing to sacrifice time, energy and money in order to win them to Christ. It means realizing we would not have been saved if Christ or other Christians had been selfish, and that we certainly cannot expect to be used by God in converting others if we are selfish.

Imitating the pattern of Christ regarding those in the second category means we must be willing to sacrifice in order to minister to their needs and build them up in the faith.

A challenging pattern

All of this leads quite naturally to the second thing we need to learn about Christ's pattern: it is a very challenging pattern.

The Christian has been delivered from the radical self-centredness of his pre-conversion days, but he is still not entirely free from self-centred living. He tries to live for the glory of God and the good of others, but he finds such living is not easy.

The truth is that the Christian is called to live out his faith in an arena in which there are all kinds of things competing for his mind. The selfless, serving, sacrificial mind of Christ asserts itself, and the Christian finds welling up within him the desire to imitate Christ's example. But suddenly other minds assert themselves as well.

The mind of Christ urges us to say 'No' to our desire for those frivolous things we don't need so we can more generously support the work of the Lord. But no sooner has the mind of the Lord spoken than we hear another mind telling us we have our rights and we are entitled to spend our money the way we want. The mind of the Lord tells us to devote time to ministering in some area of vital need, but no sooner has its sweet whisper died down than we hear the words of another mind telling us not to serve if we are not recognized and applauded.

The mind of Christ is constantly competing with the mind of selfish ambition, the mind of personal rights, the mind of fleshly gratification and the mind of carefully guarding our own interests. The Philippian Christians were evidently feeling the trauma of being caught between these competing minds because we find Paul urging them, 'Let nothing be done through selfish ambition or conceit, but in lowliness of mind let each esteem others better than himself. Let each of you look out not only for his own interests, but also for the interests of others' (vv. 3-4).

What are we to do when other minds compete with the mind of Christ? Paul says we are to 'let' the mind of Christ be in us. In other words, we are to let it have control. When the mind of Christ asserts itself we are to yield to it. When contrary minds assert themselves we are to let the mind of Christ crowd them out. Picture it like this. When we hear knocking on the door of our minds and open it to find several different ways of thinking before us, we are to let the mind of Christ in and shut the others out.

A crucial pattern

It is the difficult, challenging nature of Christ's pattern that compelled Paul to emphasize the crucial nature of the pattern set by Christ.

Paul begins this passage with a series of four statements beginning with 'if'. 'If there is any consolation in Christ, if any comfort of love, if any fellowship of the Spirit, if any affection and mercy,' then, Paul says, the Philippians are to imitate the pattern Christ demonstrated in coming to this earth.

What was he getting at? He was essentially saying this: 'You Philippians say you know Jesus Christ as your Lord and Saviour. You say you have experienced the consolation that comes from knowing you are loved by Christ. You say you know what it is to experience the mercy of God and to be in fellowship with the Spirit of God. If you have indeed experienced what you claim, you need to show it in your lives by following the pattern of Christ.'

When Christians fail to imitate the pattern of Christ and live selfishly they essentially say there is nothing to Christianity at all, that it hasn't really changed their lives.

We usually have to see how crucial something is before we pay much attention to it. We neglect our bodies until we have some serious illness. We neglect our marriages until trouble starts. We neglect our children until they break our hearts. When we finally see the importance of these things we begin to give to them the attention they deserve. So it is with following the pattern of Christ. When we see the importance of it we shall be anxious to let it control and dominate our lives. When we reflect deeply on what we owe Christ, we shall be anxious to show that he has truly made a difference in our lives. When we reflect seriously on the great needs of those who are apart from Christ, we shall be anxious to show them the difference he has made in our lives. When we reflect deeply on the great need of our fellow Christians for comforting and encouraging ministry, we shall be anxious to demonstrate the pattern of Christ in our lives. The importance of Christ's pattern, then, becomes our incentive for following it. May God himself help us to see the importance of it and to make following Christ's pattern the chief business of each day.

1. Warren Wiersbe shared this account in personal conversation.

Section V

Key words of Christmas

17.
Fulfilled!

Matthew 1-2

There is no shortage of words that pop into our minds when we hear the word 'Christmas'. 'Peace', 'joy', 'manger', 'star', 'carols', 'gifts' and a host of others spring readily to mind. Along with these words, there are lesser-known words which actually take us closer to the true meaning of Christmas than some of the better-known ones.

The word 'fulfilled' is one such word. How long would it take most of us to mention it in connection with Christmas? Yet it is one of those words that brings us to the very heart of Christmas. It did not take Matthew long to get to it in his Gospel.

His first two chapters are devoted to the birth of Christ, and they contain the phrase, 'that it might be fulfilled', a total of three times (1:22; 2:15,23). They also contain the phrases, 'Then was fulfilled...' (2:17) and 'Thus it is written by the prophet...' (2:5).

After his account of the birth of Christ, Matthew launches into a description of the life of Christ, and he again constantly employs that phrase, 'that it might be fulfilled' (4:14; 8:17; 12:17; 13:35; 21:4). And he employs it again when he comes to describe the death of Christ (27:35).

The prophecies fulfilled by the birth of Jesus

The kind of birth

Let's return to those verses in which Matthew describes the birth of Christ. What Old Testament prophecies were fulfilled on that occasion? Matthew first cites the virgin birth (1:22-23).

Joseph and Mary were betrothed when it was discovered that Mary was with child. (1:18). This was before they were married and before they had engaged in sexual relations.

While Joseph was pondering these things, an angel appeared to him with some glorious news and some instructions. The glorious news was that Mary was 'with child of the Holy Spirit' (1:18). In other words, she had conceived, not through sexual intercourse, but through an act of the Holy Spirit of God (Luke 1:35).

This act of the Holy Spirit was for the purpose of bringing into this world the Son of God so that he might 'save his people from their sins' (Matt. 1:21). And it was in keeping with what the prophet Isaiah had declared centuries before: 'Behold, the virgin shall be with child, and bear a Son, and they shall call his name Immanuel...' (Matt. 1:23, quoting Isa. 7:14).

Along with this news, Joseph received the instructions that he was to go ahead and take Mary to be his wife (1:20).

The place of birth

From that point, Matthew moves on to emphasize that Jesus was born in Bethlehem, and this was a fulfilment of the prophecy of Micah (Micah 5:2). This fulfilment was no small matter. Joseph and Mary were from Nazareth, which was over seventy miles north of the village of Bethlehem, a very significant distance in those days.

How did Joseph and Mary happen, then, to be in Bethlehem on the very night that the Lord Jesus was born? The answer is supplied for us by Luke: 'And it came to pass in those days that a decree went out from Caesar Augustus that all the world should be registered. This census first took place while Quirinius was governing Syria. So all went to be registered, everyone to his own city. Joseph also went up from Galilee, out of the city of Nazareth, into Judea, to the city of David, which is called Bethlehem, because he was of the house and lineage of David, to be registered with Mary, his betrothed wife, who was with child' (Luke 2:1-5).

Let's see, now. Out of all the times when Caesar could have issued a decree for everyone to return to his home town to be registered, he just happened to choose that time that would place Joseph and Mary in Bethlehem on that very night when Mary would give birth to Jesus and fulfil Micah's prophecy. The Holy Spirit's timing is exquisite!

The slaughter of the infants

After Jesus was born, Herod the king was enraged over the thought of having a rival king on his hands, and ordered all the male children under two years of age in and around Bethlehem to be put to death (Matt. 2:16). And Matthew observes that even that was a fulfilment of prophecy (2:17-18).

Joseph and Mary fled from Herod's wrath into Egypt and, after Herod's death, returned to Nazareth. All of this also fulfilled Old Testament prophecy (Matt. 2:13-15,19-23).

The importance of fulfilled prophecy

Why was this matter of fulfilled prophecy so important to Matthew? The answer is that he was dealing with an issue of enormous significance.

The Old Testament opens with the account of Adam and Eve falling into sin and destroying their relationship with God

(Gen. 3:1-8). But it also tells of God seeking Adam and Eve out to give them the promise of one who would come and provide a perfect atonement for their sins (Gen. 3:11-15).

Here, then, is how enormous this matter was to Matthew. The coming of the Messiah was the only possible way for sinners to be forgiven and to enter again into fellowship with God.

All through the Old Testament era men and women of faith looked forward to the time when the Messiah would come to provide the perfect atonement. God fanned their faith by sending prophets to predict details about the Messiah's birth, life and death. After these long centuries of anticipation, Jesus was born.

But was he the Messiah? Was he the one who would provide the perfect atonement that would purchase eternal salvation? Yes, he claimed to be the Son of God who came to save people from their sins, but how could they be sure he was telling the truth? Perhaps he was a deceiver, or deceived himself, or both. Matthew's answer to the question of whether Jesus was the Messiah is this: look at the prophecies.

Was Jesus the Messiah? Look at the virgin birth. Keep in mind that two of the Gospel writers affirm the virgin birth. These Gospels were written only a few years after Jesus' death. A lot of people who had been closely associated with Jesus were still alive when these Gospels began to circulate. In all probability Mary was still alive at this time. All of these people and Mary herself would have set the record straight if the accounts of a virgin birth were mere fabrications.

Luke's account of the virgin birth is especially noteworthy because he was a physician. He had the keen, analytical mind of a scientist, and would have been naturally sceptical of a virgin birth. But he gives us the more detailed account of the virgin birth!

Was Jesus the Messiah? Look at the place of his birth. The Old Testament said 'Bethlehem'. All the religious leaders convened by Herod readily agreed that Bethlehem was the place where the Messiah was to be born (Matt. 2:4-6). No one, no matter how sceptical and antagonistic towards Christianity, even bothers to dispute the fact that Jesus was born in Bethlehem.

These two fulfilments, the manner of Jesus' birth and the place of it, are impressive enough, but, as we have noted, they are only two of the many fulfilments cited by Matthew. And Matthew didn't cite all the Old Testament prophecies fulfilled by Christ. In fact, we may say the fulfilments mentioned by Matthew constitute a mere scratch on the surface when we begin to compare them to the total number of prophecies fulfilled by the Lord Jesus Christ. Josh McDowell, in his *Evidence That Demands a Verdict*, maintains that Jesus fulfilled over three hundred prophecies in all and proceeds to enumerate sixty-one of these.[1]

What is the significance of all this? There can be no doubt about the answer to that question. Jesus' detailed fulfilment of a multitude of prophecies proves beyond any shadow of a doubt that the baby whose birth we celebrate at Christmas was no ordinary baby, but he was in fact God in human flesh.

And that fact establishes this: if he was God in human flesh he, and he alone, is the way of salvation. Here is the true significance of Christmas: the long-awaited Saviour has come. The call of Christmas is for each of us to repent of our sins and receive the salvation he has provided.

1. Josh McDowell, *Evidence that Demands a Verdict,* Campus Crusade for Christ, Inc., pp.150-83.

18.
Believed!

Luke 1:5-25

After a brief introduction, the Gospel of Luke plunges us into the realm of Christmas. His first chapter tells us of the prelude to Christmas, and his second chapter tells us of Christmas itself.

As we read the events leading up to that first Christmas, it occurs to us that there is a most lamentable and terrible tragedy here. It is the tragedy of Zacharias.

Here we have a very wonderful man. He was a priest, but he was more than that. It is possible to be a religious professional and have no real regard for God or his laws. This was not the case with Zacharias. Luke tells us he and his wife were both 'righteous before God, walking in all the commandments and ordinances of the Lord blameless' (v. 6).

Zacharias and Elizabeth were godly people. They loved God. They obeyed God. They were also people who believed that God was going to keep his promise of sending a Saviour to the world. All seems to be well here. Where is the tragedy?

Luke tells us it was Zacharias' turn to serve in the temple. His duties required him to burn incense. This was a daily ritual in which the priest went very near the veil that separated the Holy Place from the Most Holy Place. Zacharias was to place the incense on the burning coals on the altar. This would cause a cloud of fragrance to arise. It represented the thanksgiving of God's people for the redemption that was theirs through the shedding of blood.

The people were outside waiting for Zacharias to return from the altar of incense. They waited and waited, but no Zacharias appeared. What had happened? Luke tells us that an angel of the Lord appeared to Zacharias while he was in the Holy Place (v. 11). That angel later identified himself as Gabriel (v. 19). The Bible tells us angels can appear to people without the individuals concerned knowing that they are angels (Heb. 13:2), but Gabriel appeared as himself because Zacharias was overwhelmed with fear (v. 12).

Gabriel had a message for Zacharias, a message that consisted of two incredible parts. The first was that Zacharias and his wife were to have a son (v. 13). The second was that this son would, in fulfilment of prophecy, prepare the way for the long-awaited Messiah (v. 17).

If we put these points together, we essentially have the angel saying this: 'Zacharias, Christmas is coming. It is so close that it may even now be considered to be Christmas Eve.' And we would expect to read that Zacharias cried out in gratitude: 'Thank you, Lord, for keeping your promise,' leaped for joy and ran out to tell the people. Instead Zacharias said to the angel, 'How shall I know this? For I am an old man, and my wife is well advanced in years' (v. 18).

The tragedy of Zacharias is, therefore, the tragedy of unbelief. And, don't forget, we're talking here about a very godly man. So we can be even more precise and say we have here the tragedy of an unbelieving believer.

Reasons for Zacharias to believe

The presence of the angel

Zacharias had every reason to believe. The fact that an angel stood right there before him should have been enough to convince him that the message was bound to come true. Angels don't just pop up every day. On top of that, he and Elizabeth had been praying for the very thing the angel announced. They had been praying God would give them a son (v. 13). Here, then, is the spectacle of a man praying for something he never expected to receive!

A *historical precedent*

Zacharias even had historical precedent to guide him and encourage him at this point. His Old Testament Scriptures, which he loved and revered, told him that his whole nation of Israel came about as the result of an old couple having a son. Abraham's body was 'as good as dead' (Heb. 11:12), and Sarah was well beyond the ability to conceive. But the Lord himself and a couple of angels dropped by one day to announce that Abraham and Sarah would indeed have a son (Gen. 18).

Zacharias knew all about this. He knew that Sarah, upon overhearing the news, broke out in laughter. And he knew the Lord had responded to Sarah's laughter by asking, 'Is anything too hard for the Lord?'

Zacharias' reason for unbelief

With all this in place, Zacharias refused to believe. We have to wonder why. And the answer is plain: Zacharias allowed what he knew about his own circumstances to override what he knew about God.

Gabriel had more work to do in order to get ready for Christmas. Later in this chapter, we find him appearing to a young woman named Mary with the message that she had been chosen to bear the Messiah (vv. 26-38). Gabriel's message to Mary placed her in a situation that was both like and unlike the situation of Zacharias. The situations were alike in that each heard a message that seemed incapable of fulfilment. While Zacharias was asked to believe that he and Elizabeth would have a son in their old age, Mary was asked to believe that she would bear a son without a human father (vv. 34-35).

The situations were different, however, in that Mary did not have as much evidence for believing as Zacharias did. While elderly people had become parents in the past, no woman had ever conceived and given birth to a child while still a virgin

Mary differed from Zacharias at another point as well. After she heard Gabriel's message, she quietly responded, 'Behold the maidservant of the Lord! Let it be to me according to your word' (v. 38).

The result of Zacharias' unbelief

But let's get back to Zacharias. Gabriel wasn't amused at his lack of faith, and he announced that Zacharias would not be able to speak until the message he refused to believe came true.

So the last thing Zacharias said for nine months was a word of doubt. When he was able to speak again, he broke into a torrent of praise to God for being faithful to his promises (vv. 67-79).

The challenge posed by Zacharias to us

We have been looking at the sad sight of an unbelieving be-liever. It is, tragically, a sight that can still be seen today.

God's people have, as Zacharias did, a clear word form God. It is right there in Scripture. Like Zacharias we have every reason to believe it but, alas, we are also like Zacharias in that we are often reluctant to believe what God clearly tells us in his Word.

Why are we so reluctant to believe God's Word? Our circumstances are such that God's Word seems implausible and impossible. Public opinion polls often seem more tangible and real than does the message of God's Word.

It is not that we totally disbelieve the Word of God. No, we believe it. It is rather a matter of degree. We don't believe it to the extent that we ought. We are believers, but we can be, if we are not careful, unbelieving believers. Zacharias speaks from the distant past about this matter. He urges all children of God to believe God fully, even when it seems foolish to do so.

Our happiness and joy as believers are in direct proportion to the greatness of our faith in the Word of God. If we have great faith, we shall know great blessedness. If we have little faith, we shall have little blessedness.

There is only one thing more tragic than the unbelieving believer, and that is the unbelieving unbeliever. God has spoken a clear word to all who are not Christians. He has spoken about your sins and your need of a Saviour. He has spoken about his Son, Jesus, as the only one who can provide salvation. He has spoken about the need to repent of your sins and place your faith and trust in Christ as the only means by which to receive this salvation.

Will you now believe this message? The unbelieving believer is still a believer and will go to heaven at last. But the unbelieving unbeliever will finally be separated from God for ever. Believers are far from perfect, but the weakest believer on this earth is in a far better position than the strongest unbeliever.

19.
Blessed!

Luke 1:26-31, 39-48

There can be no doubt that the word 'blessed' is one of the more prominent words in Luke's account of the first Christmas. When he appeared to Mary to announce that she would be the mother of the Messiah, the angel Gabriel said, 'Blessed are you among women!' (Luke 1:28). Elizabeth used the word 'blessed' three times in her words of welcome to Mary (vv. 42,45). And Mary used the word 'blessed' to describe how future generations would speak of her (v. 48).

The words 'bless', 'blessed', 'blessing' and 'blessedness' are found a great number of times throughout the Scripture. Perhaps the beatitudes come most readily to mind when we hear the word 'blessed'. (The word 'beatitude' comes from a Latin word meaning 'blessed'.)

What does it mean to be blessed? Most of us have learned that it is synonymous with happiness. Each time we see the word 'blessed' we can substitute the word 'happy' without doing any damage at all to the meaning of a particular verse. But it is possible to sharpen the definition of the word 'blessed' by saying it means to be made happy by receiving a great benefit, favour or privilege.

This was obviously true in Mary's case. She was indeed a very happy person because of the awesome privilege of being selected by God to bear the Messiah. Gabriel greeted her with these words: 'Rejoice, highly favoured one...' (v. 28). A moment later he told her she had 'found favour' with God (v. 30).

Think for a moment about the glorious benefit Mary received. God had only one Son, and out of all the women he could have chosen to bring him into this world, he chose Mary.

Mary's response to her blessedness

How did Mary respond to this inestimable privilege? How did she respond to her blessedness? She tells us in these words: 'My soul magnifies the Lord, and my spirit has rejoiced in God my Saviour...' (vv. 46-47).

Her understanding

There are a couple of things for us to note here. The first has to do with this word 'magnify'. That word, by the way, gives us the name of this 'song' of Mary, the 'Magnificat'.

What does it mean to magnify something? It means to cause an object to loom large. The whole purpose of Mary's song was to make something loom large. What was this something? In this case, it was a someone. Mary's song was designed to cause God to loom large in the minds of others. She wanted him to be held in higher esteem or respect.

There was no doubt in her mind about the reason why she had been blessed by receiving the favour of God. It was not because of her merit, but because of God's grace that had worked in her life. All the praise and honour for the glorious thing that had happened to her was, therefore, to go to the mighty, merciful God.

Her wholeheartedness

A second thing for us to note about Mary's response is the wholehearted fervour of it. She praised the Lord with her soul and rejoiced in him with her spirit (vv. 46-47). There is no nonchalant, casual half-heartedness here! The favour God had bestowed upon her was no small favour, her subsequent happiness was no small happiness and she knew, therefore, that her praise must be no small praise.

The greatness of our blessedness

We have no difficulty in seeing the blessing of Mary. Ask anyone you like if he or she considers Mary to have been given a massive favour or privilege, and that person will have no hesitation in agreeing. It is obvious. Mary was blessed. She was blessed because she had received an extraordinary benefit, but many of us have been more blessed than she. Mary's blessing was great, but many of us have received a far greater blessing.

This truth is made abundantly clear later in Luke's Gospel. The Lord Jesus Christ had just spoken some powerful words about the defeat of Satan and all his malevolent forces, and one of his hearers was so moved and touched by what he said that she spontaneously called out, 'Blessed is the womb that bore you, and the breasts which nursed you!' (Luke 11:27).

She was right. She said exactly what Gabriel and Elizabeth and Mary herself said. Mary was a happy person because of this great privilege she received. But the Lord Jesus Christ responded in these words: 'More than that, blessed are those who hear the word of God and keep it!' (Luke 11:28). He wasn't denying Mary's blessing at all, but he was concerned to point out that there are those who have been far more blessed.

Who are these more blessed people? Jesus says they are the ones who 'hear the word of God and keep it'.

Why are these people more blessed than Mary? Those who hear the Word of God and keep it have received the highest gift God has to offer: the gift of eternal life.

Have you ever made this connection between the Word of God and eternal life? We have in Scripture this Word of God, and the whole point of this Word, its purpose and design, is to convey to us the way to eternal life. Jesus himself made the connection for us by saying, 'The words that I speak to you are spirit, and they are life' (John 6:63).

The meaning of those words was not lost on Simon Peter and the other eleven disciples. While others were turning away from Jesus, these men stayed. When Jesus asked why they did not leave along with the others, Peter responded, 'Lord, to whom shall we go? You have the words of eternal life' (John 6:68).

Before we leave this point, let's make sure we understand a couple of things.

First, let's make sure we understand the greatness of the blessing of eternal life. It is life such as we have never experienced before. Everything here is rotting, withering, fading and dying, and all of that makes life here difficult and trying. But eternal life — that's different! It is life without end, but it is also life without any mixture of sadness or difficulty.

Let's also make sure we understand the means by which eternal life becomes ours. This comes as a shocking word to many, but it is crystal clear in the Bible that eternal life is not the automatic possession of all. It is only the possession of those who hear and keep the Word of God.

What does it mean to hear and keep the Word of God? There are different levels of hearing. It is possible to hear and not really hear, to hear words without really understanding their meaning and their importance. There are many who hear the Word of God in this way each and every time they come into the house of God. Yes, they hear the words of the gospel, and if they were asked to give the gist of what was said, they would have no difficulty in doing so. But they have not really heard. They have not understood that this gospel is talking about them and their own happiness. It tells them they must stand before a holy God and give account of themselves. It tells them they must be holy even as he is holy before they can be acceptable to him. It tells them there is no way for them to have that holiness he demands apart from the Lord Jesus Christ. It tells them to receive the Lord Jesus as their Lord and Saviour by repenting of their sins and placing their faith and trust in him. It tells them that Christ can make them new creatures, and that newness will be reflected in their lives by the desire to live for Christ and keep his commandments.

The real test of whether a person has truly heard the message of eternal life is whether he or she has acted on these truths that are so clearly laid out in the Word of God. All those who are Christians have heard the Word of God, acted upon it, received God's gift of eternal life and are, therefore, more blessed than Mary was in being selected to bear Jesus. By the way, Mary herself enjoyed this greater blessing. She trusted that one whom she bore to be her sin-bearer and received the greatest of all gifts, the gift of eternal life.

Our response to our blessedness

In the light of these things, there are two questions of supreme importance for us to ask. Those of us who have received that greatest of all privileges — that privilege that far surpasses the privilege bestowed upon Mary when she was selected to bear Jesus — must ask ourselves if we are responding appropriately to it.

My point is this: if Mary's lesser gift caused her to magnify the Lord with all her heart, the greater gift of eternal life should cause us to be magnifying the Lord to an even greater degree. Are we doing so? Do we find praise for our salvation welling up within us each day? When we come together for worship, do we worship from the heart, or are we nonchalant, casual and distracted in worship? One way to magnify God is by keeping his commandments. Are we doing this?

There is also a question for those who have not received that greatest blessing God has to bestow: why not? An old song put it so well:

There is a cross where the Saviour died:
His blood flowed out in a crimson tide,
A sacrifice for the sins of men,
And free to all who will enter in.
Then why will ye die? Oh, why will ye die?
When the crimson cross is so near by,
Oh, why will ye die?

20.
Marvelled!

Luke 2:8-18

To marvel is to be astonished or amazed at some strange or unusual phenomenon. It is to be filled with a sense of wonder and awe over something that is of an extraordinary nature.

We all need to marvel from time to time. It is good for us. It makes life richer and more meaningful to stand in awe of something. We all need to be reminded from time to time that there are realities much larger than ourselves.

We have trouble marvelling today. It is not that we don't marvel at anything, but rather that we marvel at things that are really not all that important, while we remain unmoved and unawed in the face of those realities that are truly awesome. We may call this the problem of 'misplaced marvelling'.

Here is an example. We marvel at things that men and women do with regularity. Take great feats in sporting action. How often we proclaim such things as 'awesome'! But great sporting feats happen all the time.

Let me give you another example from the realm of Christmas itself. We can 'Ooh!' and 'Ah!' at beautiful lighting displays, or elaborate Christmas pageants. Is there anything wrong with that? Not necessarily. The question is, do we understand that there is much more in Christmas of an awesome nature than lights and pageants.

As Luke wraps up his account of the first Christmas, he makes mention of people marvelling, and these people did not suffer at this point from the problem of 'misplaced marvelling'. On the contrary, this original Christmas marvelling was of the truest kind. It was right for these people to marvel.

What were they marvelling at? Luke says they marvelled at 'those things which were told them by the shepherds' (Luke 2:18).

The marvelling of the shepherds

These shepherds had engaged in some marvelling themselves. There they were, keeping watch over their flocks in the fields outside Bethlehem, when their night-time reverie was suddenly shattered. An angel of the Lord abruptly appeared before them. They were at first terrified, but the angel quickly assured them that they not only had nothing to fear, but rather had great reason to rejoice. The long-awaited, eagerly anticipated Messiah had been born that very night in Bethlehem. The angel put it in these words: 'Do not be afraid, for behold, I bring you good tidings of great joy which will be to all people. For there is born to you this day in the city of David a Saviour, who is Christ the Lord' (vv. 10-11).

That was in and of itself marvellous enough, but there was more to come. Suddenly a whole host of angels burst from the darkness of the heavens to praise God with these words: 'Glory to God in the highest, and on earth peace, goodwill toward men' (v. 14).

The next thing we are told is that the shepherds went to Bethlehem to see this marvellous thing of which the angel had spoken. They came 'with haste' to that humble stable and found Joseph, Mary and the baby (v. 16). I can see them standing there in the shadows drinking in that sight. It was one they would never forget. And it was one they could not keep to themselves. With sheer delight these men made 'widely known' what the angel had said (v. 17) and, we may be sure, what they themselves had seen.

Perhaps someone is saying, 'Well, if I had seen and heard a whole band of angels, I would have marvelled too.' But while the shepherds indeed marvelled, we are told that all those who heard their story marvelled as well (v. 18). In other words, people who had not themselves seen or heard the angels marvelled at what had taken place. If those people who received an account of those events marvelled, we who have ourselves received an account of these things should marvel as well.

And that should cause us to ask if we have indeed marvelled over Christmas. Have we marvelled over the account that we have here in the Scriptures? No, I'm not talking about marvelling over the fact of angels appearing to ordinary men, although that is marvellous enough. I'm talking rather about marvelling over Christmas itself. I'm talking about marvelling over the same thing those people marvelled at in Luke's account, namely, what the shepherds said. And what did the shepherds say? They related what the angels had said to them (v. 17).

Here then is the true marvel of Christmas: 'For there is born to you this day in the city of David a Saviour, who is Christ the Lord' (v. 11). Have you marvelled at it?

Three marvels

That Jesus should come at all

As I look more closely at the angel's statement, I have to say I find three central marvels in the Christmas message. First, I am amazed at the fact of Jesus' coming at all.

The Bible tells us the Lord Jesus did not have his beginning that night at Bethlehem, that he is without beginning and without end. Prior to his coming here, he existed with God and was equal to God. The apostle John says of him, 'In the beginning was the Word, and the Word was with God, and the Word was God. He was in the beginning with God' (John 1:1-2).

In order to come to us, he had to leave all the glories of heaven. Because the gap between the Creator and the created order is so staggeringly large, it would have been marvellous enough had he left heaven to come to a perfect humanity on a perfect earth. But it was to no perfect humanity and no perfect earth that he came. The Bible tells us all had become corrupt and defiled through sin.

So the chasm he crossed was infinitely greater than the great gap between the Creator and the created. It was nothing less than the gap between the holy, undefiled God and unholy, defiled sinners. Who can measure the greatness of that gap?

Think of it in these terms. Here is a king sitting on his throne. He is surrounded by beauty. He is honoured and revered by his servants. His robe is of the finest fabric. His sceptre sparkles with jewels and glitters with gold. He looks out of the window of his palace and sees one of his subjects fall into a deep pit. He rises from his throne, lays down his sceptre, strips off his robe, leaves the palace, leaps into the pit and lifts the man out.

Would not such a thing be a marvellous sight? Multiply it ten thousand times ten thousand, and you begin to have the faintest of glimmers into what Christmas is about. It is about a king leaving the finery, the glories and the praises of heaven to plunge into the pit of sin and condemnation so that he might help his subjects out.

That Jesus should come in the way he did

It would have been amazing enough had Jesus just swooped down from heaven as God to walk with us here on earth. But the Bible says he did something far greater than that. He became one of us! And he did not simply come as a full-grown man, but rather as a mere baby in a manger.

Why did he do it? The author of Hebrews supplies the answer. He says, 'Inasmuch then as the children have partaken of flesh and blood, he himself likewise shared in the same, that through death he might destroy him who had the power of death, that is, the devil... Therefore, in all things he had to be make like his brethren' (Heb. 2:14,17).

The point is clear. In order to do something for us Jesus had to be completely like us. He could not have represented humankind if he had not been fully human, and men and women do not swoop down from the sky. They are born. So Jesus was born.

That Jesus should come to do what he did

But what was this thing he had to do for us? That brings me to a third amazing thing about Christmas. It would have been amazing enough had Jesus just come to this earth as a man. As a man, he could have instructed us by his words and by his example. He could have encouraged us. He could have sympathized with us. But the Bible tells us he did something that far surpasses all that.

He came into the midst of our sin and condemnation to deliver us from the same and to restore us to fellowship with God. Instruction, encouragement and sympathy were not sufficient for this high task. The only way for us to be released from sin was for the penalty incurred by sin to be paid. That penalty was eternal death. Here is the thing that I marvel at most — Jesus Christ went there to Calvary's cross and received in his own person an eternity of separation from God. And all those who now repent of their sins and embrace him as their Lord and Saviour do not have to pay that penalty themselves.

Marvel if you please at the mere trivialities of life in general and Christmas in particular, but, by the grace of God, I will marvel at the glorious sight of one who came all the way from heaven's glory to earth's sin and shame, who came as a man and who came to die in my stead. Yes, this Christmas and every Christmas I will marvel at the message of the angel: 'For there is born to you this day in the city of David a Saviour, who is Christ the Lord.'

Section VI

What makes Christmas special

21.

A special kind of baby

Matthew 1:18-25

What makes Christmas special? It is not friends and family, trees and gifts, lights and carols. The thing that makes Christmas special is that it celebrates the birth of a special baby.

All babies are special in a sense. I shall never forget the joy of seeing my two baby boys for the first time, which was followed by the joy of holding them, which was followed by the joys of changing nappies and getting up in the middle of the night!

Yes, all babies are special, but there never has been and never will be a baby like the one whose birth we celebrate on Christmas Day.

Born in a special way

What made Jesus such a special baby? First, the manner of his birth (Matt. 1:18-20).

Mary was engaged to be married to Joseph, but before they were married, and while she was still a virgin, Matthew says, 'She was found [to be] with child of the Holy Spirit' (v. 18).

This immediately cast Joseph into a deep dilemma because engagement was far more serious and binding than it is today. Even though they had not begun living together, Joseph and

Mary had pledged themselves to each other in the presence of witnesses. This betrothal was such a serious matter that a woman who proved unfaithful during this time was punishable by death (Deut. 22:23-24).

Joseph, a fine and sensitive man, wanted to do nothing to hurt Mary. He decided, therefore, to just quietly divorce her instead of resorting to the legal channels. Before he could carry out his plan, God graciously intervened and disclosed to him why Mary was with child (v. 20). So Joseph learned the truth about Mary in much the same way that Mary learned about it herself (Luke 1:26-38).

In addition to this, Joseph was informed that this was the fulfilment of the prophecy of Isaiah: 'Behold, the virgin shall be with child, and bear a son...' (vv. 22-23; Isa. 7:14).

So Jesus was a special baby because he was born in a special way — he was born of a virgin, born without a human father.

This has always been one of the favourite targets of people who enjoy trying to discredit the Bible. They scoff at such a thing on the grounds that it is impossible. Their argument seems to be that this could not happen; therefore it did not happen.

Surely there is no better answer to these critics than the answer the angel Gabriel gave to Mary when she asked, 'How can this be, since I am a virgin?' (Luke 1:34, marginal reading). Part of Gabriel's reply was: 'For with God nothing will be impossible' (Luke 1:37).

I confess I am always a bit amused by people who claim to believe in God and who still have trouble accepting the miracles recorded in the Bible. God, by definition, is unlimited in power. Why, then, should we stumble at the miracles which exhibit his power? I have always felt that if one accepts the opening words of the Bible, 'In the beginning God...', one should have no trouble accepting anything that follows.

Born for a special work

But the manner of his birth doesn't exhaust the uniqueness of Jesus. We must go on to see the purpose of his birth (Matt. 1:21-25).

Joseph was told to name this special baby Jesus, 'for he will save his people from their sins' (v. 21). The word 'Jesus' literally means, 'Jehovah is salvation.' But what does the word 'salvation' mean? It means to be delivered or emancipated. And from what do people need to be delivered? The answer is clearly given by the angel — 'from their sins'.

This is the work Jesus came to do. When he was ready to begin his public ministry, John the Baptist hailed him with the words: 'Behold! The Lamb of God who takes away the sin of the world!' (John 1:29). Jesus himself was to say, 'For the Son of Man has come to seek and to save that which was lost' (Luke 19:10).

Perhaps you are wondering if sin is really all that serious. The answer is a resounding, 'Yes!' We are quite content to gloss over our sins, and even to crack jokes bout them, but God is holy and he cannot lightly dismiss sin. If you want to get an idea of how holy God is all you have to do is read the Ten Commandments. There you find what he demands of each of us. He not only demands that our actions be pure, but that also our thoughts and words be clean.

Many today are inclined to respond to this by saying something like: 'What is it to me if God is holy and doesn't like how I am living? It's my life and I can do as I please. If God doesn't like it, that's his problem!'

I assure you, it is not that easy. You see, this God who demands holiness has the power to bring each one of us into judgement. In fact, he has promised to do exactly that (Heb. 9:27; Acts 17:30-31), and if we stand before him in all our sins, he will cast us into eternal destruction (2 Thess. 1:9).

The only way we can stand before this holy God without fear is to make sure our sins are forgiven, that we are delivered, or saved, from them. Is there any way our sins can be dealt with and taken out of the way? Yes, thank God, there is. This holy God who had promised to judge sinners is also a gracious God who desires to forgive us our sins, and he has made a way of salvation for us in and through the Lord Jesus Christ. Jesus Christ, by becoming a man, came under the same demands that God has placed on all men. Paul says, 'But when the fulness of the time had come, God sent forth his Son, born of a woman, born under the law…' (Gal. 4:4).

But whereas we had utterly and completely failed to keep God's law, Jesus kept it. He didn't sin in thought, word, or deed. After he had rendered complete obedience to the law, he went to the cross and there received in his own body the wrath of God in the place of guilty sinners (1 Peter 2:24). By his perfect life and sacrificial death, he provided all who receive him with a complete salvation. By his life he provided the righteousness we need to stand before God, and by his death he paid for the sins we have committed.

How do we receive Christ? We must recognize we are sinners, turn from our sins and trust in what he did as the complete and only hope of salvation.

Now we are in a position to see why the virgin birth of Christ was so necessary. Jesus Christ had to become a man in order to save us, but at the same time he had to be different from us. If he had not been born of a virgin, he would have been just like us. He would have been a sinner himself and would have had to pay for his own sins. He would, therefore, have been completely unable to help us.

S. G. DeGraaf puts it like this: 'On the one hand he is of the flesh and blood of Mary and therefore one of us. On the other hand, he is without human ancestry for he is conceived by the Holy Spirit. He is the Holy One, a stranger to sin.'[1]

In short, the only way we could be saved is through one who was fully God and fully man. We needed someone who could identify with us and represent us without becoming a sinner himself. This Jesus did. The virgin birth allowed for identification with the sinner without the contamination of sin.

The question before us is how to respond to this special baby of Christmas. Joseph was called upon to accept a child that was not his own. In a sense we are all faced with the same choice. Christ, even though he was a real man, was still different from all men in that he was not a sinner. Will you now accept this one who is different from us as the only hope for your salvation? Will you accept this stranger to sin as the only Saviour from sin?

1. S. G. DeGraaf, *Promise and Deliverance,* vol. iii, Presbyterian and Reformed Publishing Co., p.26.

22.

A special kind of king

Matthew 2:1-6

Christmas is special because it celebrates the birth of a special baby, but that is only part of the story. That baby in the manger was also a king.

Most people are quite comfortable with the baby Jesus in the manger. They are prepared to allow the baby Jesus a part in the Christmas pageantry. Perhaps they even feel some kind of sentimental attachment to him. But mention Christ as a king on a throne, and a lot of these people become uneasy. Baby Jesus in the manger is not perceived by most as a threat, but King Jesus on a throne — that's a different story! You see, kingship implies authority, and if there is anything that unnerves modern man, it is authority.

But this is an issue that cannot be ignored. Whether we like it or not, Jesus Christ is a king. In fact, he is a special kind of king: he is 'King of kings and Lord of lords' (Rev. 19:16). Ignore this King and you most certainly invite his wrath!

The opening verses of Matthew 2 give us some glimpses into the kingship of Christ and what made it special.

A king who attracted others

First, we see that Christ was a king who attracted others, but not his own people. Immediately this passage introduces us to the magi from the East who arrived in Jerusalem and began saying, 'Where is he who has been born King of the Jews? For we have seen his star in the East and have come to worship him' (v. 2).

There has been a good deal of conjecture about these men, and we shall look at them in more detail later. For now let's take note of the fact that, from the very first, Jesus had tremendous appeal to the Gentiles. These men were the first of an innumerable host of Gentiles who would bow in adoration before him.

How different was the response of Herod and the Jews! Herod himself was not a Jew, but as their king he was the representative of the whole nation. Herod himself trembled with fear as he contemplated the possibility of his throne passing over to this new king. His only concern was to rid himself of this threat as quickly as possible. His sin-darkened mind was not capable of comprehending the futility of fighting against the king whom God had long promised and finally sent.

Hurriedly, Herod called in the chief priests and scribes to determine where the long-awaited Messiah was to be born. These men had no trouble in answering his question. They knew all about the Messianic prophecies of the Old Testament, and they knew these prophecies included a word from Micah that the Messiah would be born in Bethlehem. But the striking thing about these religious leaders is their indifference to the possibility that their Messiah had finally arrived. They answered Herod's question in an indifferent fashion and then went on their way. They showed absolutely no interest in going with the magi to see if the prophecies had been fulfilled.

This is certainly an unusual turn of events. When an heir to a throne is born we expect his own people to rejoice. Other nations might take note of the birth of the heir and might even express some joy over it, but we do not expect other nations to react to the heir with the same joy and jubilation as the heir's own nation. And yet this is what happened when Jesus was born. While the magi traversed a vast distance and faced various dangers to worship this new king, the leaders of Israel took scant notice of it at all.

The apostle John summarizes this unusual part of Christ's kingship by saying of Christ, 'He came to his own, and his own people did not receive him' (John 1:11, marginal reading). Happily, John didn't stop there but went on to add, 'But as many as received him, to them he gave the right to become children of God, to those who believe in his name...' (John 1:12). That includes even Gentiles!

A king who fulfilled prophecy

Notice, in the next place, that Jesus was special because he was a king who fulfilled prophecy.

No other king comes close to Jesus in this area. Some biblical kings fulfilled one or two predictions made concerning their reigns, but Jesus fulfilled all the prophecies made in the Old Testament concerning the Messiah. Josh McDowell says, 'The Old Testament written over a 1,500 year period contains several hundred references to the coming Messiah. All of these were fulfilled in Christ and they establish a solid confirmation of his credentials as the Messiah.'[1]

McDowell proceeds to list fifteen prophecies that Jesus fulfilled in his birth alone! Do you have any idea of what a staggering thing that is? Then top it off by adding all the prophecies Jesus fulfilled in his life, death, burial and resurrection. You can toss around computations of this probability until your head swims, but the bottom line is this: Jesus Christ had to be God himself! There is no other way he could have fulfilled all these prophecies.

Some critics have argued that Jesus' fulfilment of prophecy was deliberate, that he found out what the prophecies were and then orchestrated a fulfilment of them. But how does one deliberately plan the place of one's birth or fulfil fourteen other prophecies at birth?

Matthew makes much of the fact that Jesus fulfilled prophecies. In this chapter alone he specifically says four times that Jesus fulfilled prophecy (vv. 5-6,15,17-18,23). Add those to the fulfilment he mentioned in the first chapter (1:22-23), and you have early in this Gospel an impressive amount. But Matthew doesn't stop there. He keeps holding this thing before his readers. Matthew's Gospel has been called 'the Gospel of the King'. He wrote to prove that Jesus was Israel's king, and he resorted, therefore, to emphasizing these many fulfilments of prophecy. When you finish reading Matthew's Gospel you have either to deliberately ignore the mountain of evidence he presents, or to take your place alongside the magi, bowing in worship before the King of Kings.

A king who was to rule in a special way

Let me point to one more indication that Jesus' kingship was special. This passage shows us that he was a king who would rule in a special way.

When the chief priests and scribes answered Herod's question they quoted from the prophet Micah, who said that out of Bethlehem would come 'a Ruler, who will shepherd my people Israel' (Matt. 2:6). Jesus, then, was to rule in a special way, as one would care for sheep. As we saw in an earlier chapter, the shepherd's job was to provide his sheep with food and water and to protect them from danger. The 23rd Psalm makes these two tasks explicitly clear. In verses 1-3, the shepherd is presented as the one who provides for the sheep, and in verse 4 he is presented as the protector of the sheep. And who is the shepherd in that best-loved psalm? We all know the answer. The psalm begins with the words: 'The Lord is my shepherd.'

So here in Matthew's Gospel we have two truths about

Jesus tied together: he is a king and he is a shepherd. He was to go about his kingly work in a shepherd-like way. Or, we might say, he was to combine a king's authority with a shepherd's heart.

I do not need to tell you how this puts Jesus in a class by himself. So many rulers have been tyrants who looked upon their subjects as merely existing for their own pleasure. Just look at Herod in this passage. What a bloodthirsty, cruel tyrant! In order to guard his own interests, he conducted a systematic search and slaughter of the infants under two years old in and around Bethlehem (Matt. 2:16-18). No wonder Matthew says when Herod was troubled all Jerusalem was troubled along with him! (v. 3).

Perhaps someone will argue that not all kings are like Herod. This is amply proven by the good kings of the Old Testament like David, but Jesus is still a special king because, even though David had a shepherd's heart, he was not able to provide for and protect his people as Christ does. He could not free his people from all wants, let alone walk through the valley of the shadow of death with them, or prepare an eternal dwelling-place for them. The reason we have the 23rd Psalm is that David recognized that there was a special Shepherd who was greater than he could ever be.

So Jesus Christ is a special king, one who combined appeal to a people not his own with a minute fulfilment of prophecy and a shepherdly kind of rule. No other king even comes close. His kingship confronts each of us with a monumental decision: will we bow in humble submission to him? Herod and the religious leaders of Jerusalem were confronted with this special kind of king and were called upon to accept him as their own. They failed. Now what will you do with this special king?

1. Josh McDowell, *Evidence that Demands a Verdict,* Campus Crusade for Christ, Inc., p.147.

23

A special kind of wisdom

Matthew 2:1-11

Christmas is special because it celebrates the birth of a special baby, a baby who was destined to be a special king. All this was the result of a special wisdom at work.

We are accustomed to hearing the wise men praised. In recent years one of the more popular Christmas slogans has been: 'Wise men still seek him!' That certainly contains an element of truth and I have no desire to minimize it, but it does seem to give too much credit to the wise men. I suggest there was a higher wisdom at work on that first Christmas than the wisdom of the magi. In fact I would go so far as to say that their wisdom failed them and they were completely cast upon God's wisdom!

Happily, we do not have to depend on our own wisdom to find the true meaning of Christmas. God's wisdom resides in the Christmas message, and it is our duty to renounce all dependence on our own wisdom and to rest in God's wisdom.

The inadequacy of human wisdom

Each Christmas the story of the wise men is depicted in the same way. These men supposedly saw an unusual star while still in their homeland and continued to follow it until it stood over the Christ child in the manger. Most of us know there is one great flaw in that depiction. The wise men had to travel a great distance, and they didn't arrive in Bethlehem on the night Jesus was born but some time well after that. When they finally got to Bethlehem they found Jesus and his parents in a house (Matt. 2:11). Some think the visit of the wise men may have occurred as much as two years after Jesus was born.

I want to address another flaw in the common understanding of the wise men, namely, the idea that they followed a spectacular star all the way from the east to Bethlehem. If the star was guiding them each step of the way, why was it necessary for them to go and enquire of Herod concerning the whereabouts of the new king? (vv. 1-2). The answer is that they were looking for information and they viewed Herod as the most likely source.

What, then, actually happened with these wise men? Who were they and how did they finally come to the Christ child?

One of the key things to remember in trying to understand these men is that they were astrologers from the East. This is what the word 'magi' means. It was their work to study the stars and make calculations and observations based on what they saw in the stars.

As they were studying the stars one night they took note of a special star and concluded from it that a great king had been born somewhere in Judea. E. E. Ellis says of them, 'Apparently they were non-Jewish religious astrologers who, from astronomical observations, inferred the birth of a great Jewish king.'[1]

S. G. DeGraaf adds, 'The wise men saw a special star or a special phenomenon in the starry heavens. As true heathen astrologers they started calculating and concluded that a special king must have been born among the Jews. They went to

Jerusalem to find out whether their calculations were correct. To a considerable extent, the wise men were pursuing their own interests by making this journey; they wanted to confirm the accuracy of their science.'[2]

Armed with their calculations, they set out for Jerusalem, the capital of Judea and the most likely place for this king to be born. After arriving there, they went to Herod as the person most likely to know about this king. Thus far their own wisdom had guided them, but it could guide them no farther.

The necessity of divine wisdom

That brings me to observe, in the second place, the absolute necessity of divine wisdom. Herod himself did not have the answer to the enquiry of the magi, but he called for the chief priests and scribes, who quoted the prophecy of Micah that the Christ would be born in Bethlehem (vv. 5-6). Herod relayed this message to the wise men (vv. 7-8).

As they set out for the village of Bethlehem they saw something astonishing: the very star they had seen back in their homeland (v. 9). A careful reading of this passage clearly reveals that they saw this star in the East (v. 2), they journeyed to Jerusalem, heard the message of the Scriptures and then, and only then, did they again see the star. The idea that they followed the star all the way to Bethlehem is simply not borne out by Scripture.

What are we to gather from all this, if not that their own wisdom was inadequate? They had to have the Word of God to direct them. It is important to notice that the star reappeared after they heard God's Word. In doing so, it served as a sign of confirmation for the Word of God. When the star thus appeared in confirmation of what they had heard, we may

be sure they ceased trusting their own calculations and believed the Word of God.

I can do no better at this point than quote S. G. DeGraaf
again: 'Not until they came to Jerusalem and talked with the
Israelites were the wise men given further guidance. They discovered that nothing was known about the birth of the king,
until they heard about the promise of the Messiah. This brought
about a change in their thinking. Their heathen wisdom had
not led them to Christ. Their own line of reasoning was inter-
rupted and the Word of promise in Israel began to guide them.'[3]

It is the same with us. Our own wisdom is inadequate.
Approach Christmas in your own wisdom and the meaning of
it will escape you. Try to understand the things of God without God's Word and you will utterly fail. The simple fact is
that man, left to his own wisdom, will never be able to arrive
at the true knowledge of God. The only way he will ever know
God is through God's graciously revealing himself, as he has
actually done in Scripture. The apostle Paul declares, 'For the
wisdom of this world is foolishness with God' (1 Cor. 3:19).

The outcome of divine wisdom

When these wise men received the Word of promise and ceased
relying on their calculation three things happened.

Finding Christ

First, they found the Christ child (Matt. 2:9). If you and I are
to find Christ we must look to God's Word. There are many
false Christs around. Everywhere we hear voices saying, 'Here
is Christ,' and 'There is Christ.' What are we to do? We are to
look into God's Word. If anyone presents a Christ to you other

than the Christ of Scripture, you may be sure it is a false Christ. Beware of the Christ who is presented as nothing more than a good teacher. Beware of the Christ who is nothing more than a mover of the emotions! Beware of the Christ who is guaranteed to make everyone healthy and wealthy!

Experiencing joy

Secondly, these wise men experienced great joy (v. 10). There is joy in coming to the end of your own wisdom and resting in God's wisdom. There is joy in knowing that man is not the measure of all things, that there is something higher and greater than we are. But what joy is there in looking at all the complex problems that refuse to yield to human wisdom and thinking this is all there is?

Worshipping Christ

Finally, these men worshipped the Christ child (v. 11). They presented first themselves ('fell down and worshipped him') and then their gifts. Gold is often associated with royalty in Scripture. Frankincense (pure incense) was offered by priests to God. Myrrh was a perfume used for anointing one's person and for burial. The nature of these gifts prompted Origen to say the magi brought 'gold, as to a king, myrrh, as to one who was mortal; and incense, as to God'.[4]

Worship is the natural outcome of finding the truth about Christ. If you do not feel like worshipping Christ, it is safe to say you have never learned the truth about him, or you are still resisting the truths you have heard. Maybe you are still trying to judge these truths by your own wisdom. Accept God's wisdom. Trust what God says in his Word about Christ and you will be constrained to join these wise men in worship.

A challenge to the reader

We have been looking at the question of what makes Christmas special. Matthew's Gospel shows us Christmas is special because of a special kind of baby, a special kind of king and a special kind of wisdom. Joseph was called upon to embrace a different kind of baby. The Jews were called upon to embrace a different kind of king. The wise men were called upon to embrace a different kind of wisdom.

Christmas confronts us with these very same issues. Christmas reminds us Jesus was a special baby, a special king and the product of a special wisdom. The great question we each must face is what to do with this Christ? The options are clearly laid out for us in Matthew's account. Joseph embraced the different, special baby he was confronted with. Herod and the Jewish leaders refused to embrace the special kind of king they were confronted with. And the wise men embraced the special kind of wisdom they were confronted with.

Christmas brings the special Christ before us again. Where do you stand? Have you taken the side of Joseph and the wise men, or have you sided with Herod and the Jewish leaders? Have you received Jesus Christ as your Lord and Saviour, or have you rejected him? May God help you even now to embrace Christ as God in the flesh, as your rightful King and as the very wisdom of God.

1. E. E. Ellis, 'Magi', in *The New Bible Dictionary,* J. D. Douglas, ed., William B. Eerdmans Publishing Company, p.765.
2. S. G. DeGraaf, *Promise and Deliverance,* vol. iii, Presbyterian and Reformed Pulbishing Co., p.31.
3. As above, pp.31-2.
4. William Hendriksen, *New Testament Commentary: Matthew,* Baker Book House, p.173.

Section VII

The King is born

24.
This king is a stranger!

John 1:9-13; Hebrews 7:26-27

Christmas is the time when Christians celebrate the birth of the greatest king of all times, Jesus Christ.

When we think of kings certain things quite naturally come to mind. We think, for instance, of someone who has absolute authority over a distinct group of people. This person is enormously rich, and he indulges himself to the fullest with extravagant living. (We still hear advertisements of products that will help us to live like a king.) This person is always surrounded with servants who answer to his beck and call. Quite often, we think of a king as someone who wields his authority without much rhyme or reason and without the slightest regard to the welfare of his subjects.

As we examine the kingship of Jesus during this Christmas season, we are going to discover he is nothing at all like the typical king. In this chapter, I want to call your attention to Jesus as a stranger. Perhaps you have never thought of him in this way. The hymn-writer Mary MacDonald expressed it like this:

Child in the manger,
Infant of Mary,
Outcast and stranger,
Lord of all.

The Scriptures above reveal two distinct ways in which Jesus may be regarded as a stranger.

Defying expectations

First, he was a stranger to his own people in that he defied their expectations.

The Jews were definitely looking for a king. Make no mistake about that. They knew their Scriptures, and those Scriptures were steeped with prophecies about a coming king. The book of Deuteronomy assured them that a prophet like Moses would arise (Deut. 18:15,18). King David, their greatest hero, had been given marvellous promises that a great king would arise from his descendants (2 Sam. 7:12-13,16). Their prophets had punctuated their prophecies with promises of the coming of this king, and with intoxicating descriptions of the glory he would bring to Israel (e.g. Amos 9:11-15; Hag. 2:6-9; Zech. 14:1-21).

The people longed for this king to come. The glory days of Israel had now faded into the distant past and not even one prophet had arisen in the last four hundred years to trumpet afresh the promise. We might interpret this combination of events to mean that the people were ready to give up all hope, but it seemed to cause many of them to cling even more tenaciously to the promises and yearn more intensely for them to be fulfilled.

More than that, the people believed the time was right for their king to come. As the New Testament era dawned they found themselves buckling under the heavy, iron heel of the Roman Empire. If their king was waiting for the best possible moment to show himself, this would seem to qualify.

One would think such circumstances would have caused them to be very responsive to the ministry of the Lord Jesus

Christ, especially in view of the fact that it clearly had the signature of the supernatural upon it. But they were not in the least bit receptive. In the words of the apostle John, 'He came to his own, and his own did not receive him' (John 1:11). Irony of ironies! He is the one who made the world (John 1:3). He is the one who gives the light of reason and conscience to every man in the world (John 1:9). He is the one of whom ample witness was borne by John the Baptist (John 1:6-8). He is the one who came not just to the world in general but to his own, the very people who had been the recipients of all the promises. And with it all, he was rejected and crucified!

How could such a thing happen? The answer is that Jesus did not live up to the people's preconceived notions about what their king would be like. They expected him to burst upon the scene, start gathering followers by making blistering speeches against the Romans and all the other Gentile 'dogs', use his supernatural powers to throw off their bondage and take Israel to a level that would surpass their golden age under David and Solomon.

But Jesus came on the scene by denouncing, not the Romans and all the injustices they had perpetrated upon the Jews, but the sins of his very own people. He launched a blistering attack on them instead of the Romans! He had the audacity to say they needed to repent of their sins and accept him as their Lord and Saviour. He added insult to injury by saying his kingdom was never intended to be of this world, but it was to be a spiritual kingdom that would be established in the hearts of all those who truly follow him.

For a while the people gave him space to rethink his position, come to his senses and make a mid-course correction, but when it finally became apparent that he was dead-set on this spiritual business, they consented to the crucifixion planned for him by the religious leaders.

And when it was all over they probably went back to their homes, shook their heads over the day's events and muttered, 'What a strange one that Jesus was!'

When we say someone is strange we usually mean he or she is in some way different from ourselves. We all have the tendency to think we are the normal ones. So it was with these people. They thought they were the normal ones and Jesus was the strange one. So they rejected him.

Undefiled by sin

But we are incorrect if we conclude from this that Jesus was a stranger only so far as the Jews were concerned. He was, and is, a stranger to all of us by nature because we are defiled by sin, but he was not. This is what Joseph Cook had in mind when he wrote:

> Gentle Mary laid her child,
> Lowly in a manger;
> There he lay, the undefiled,
> To the world a stranger.

This is the truth brought home to us by the author of Hebrews. Jesus, he says, was 'holy, harmless, undefiled, separate from sinners...' (Heb. 7:26).

We hear so much at this time of the year about Jesus becoming one of us that we leap to the conclusion that he was just exactly like us. We may even feel the temptation to excuse sin, by telling ourselves that since Jesus became one of us, he understands. The author of Hebrews makes it clear that Christ can sympathize with us because he 'was in all points tempted as we are', but he adds that Christ was 'without sin' (Heb. 4:15).

We must always remember that Jesus became like us, but not totally like us. Yes, let's take comfort from the fact that because he became one of us, he understands the human experience. But let's take even more comfort from the fact that he became one of us so that he could do something for us — namely, provide the redemption we could not provide for ourselves.

This truth is forcefully driven home in several Scriptures. The apostle John declares, 'And you know that he was manifested to take away our sins, and in him there is no sin' (1 John 3:5). And Paul says Christ, even though he knew no sin, was 'made ... sin for us, that we might become the righteousness of God in him' (2 Cor. 5:21).

This much ought to be clear to each and every one of us: Jesus could not have provided redemption for us if he had received the same sinful nature we have. Now we are in a position to see why the virgin birth of Christ was necessary. Jesus Christ had to become a man in order to save us. But at the same time he had to be different from us. If he had not been born of a virgin, he would have been just like us. He would have been a sinner himself and thus wholly unable to help us.

In short, the only way we could be saved is through one who was fully God and fully man. We needed someone to identify with us and represent us without becoming a sinner himself. This Jesus did.

When the angel appeared to Joseph, he asked him to embrace a baby that was not his own, to embrace this strange baby who was supernaturally conceived. I have a similar question to ask each of you. Have you received this one who was a stranger to his own and a stranger to sin as the King of your life? That is the great question this Christmas message confronts us with. Here is the marvellous thing — if you will bow before him in repentance and faith and own him as your rightful Sovereign, you will find he is no longer a stranger but the most wonderful friend you could ever know. This Christmas season will go down as the greatest in your life if you will make it your time to embrace the King of kings as your personal King.

25.
This king is a servant!

Matthew 10:24-25; 20:25-28; Philippians 2:5-11

It is not too far-fetched to imagine a king who is a stranger to the people over whom he rules. But who can conceive of a king being a servant? It is like talking about a giant pygmy or a square circle. The two simply don't belong together. Everyone knows kings are not to serve, but are to be served.

Jesus Christ is not a typical king, and the Bible makes it clear he came to be a servant. He said it himself: 'The Son of Man did not come to be served, but to serve...' (Matt. 20:28).

How can such a thing be? Jesus is such a great king that the Scriptures actually call him 'King of kings' (1 Tim. 6:15). If he is the greatest of all kings, how can he be a servant?

Let's stop and think about servants for a moment. What immediately comes to mind when you hear that word? Do you not think of someone who has work to do? Do you not think of someone who is under authority and who has no will of his own, but simply does the work assigned to him? Do you not think of someone who has little or none of the world's goods, lowly circumstances and no status? Do you not picture someone whose life involves suffering, pain and sorrow?

Do you agree these are the major characteristics of the servant? You will find, then, that all of the characteristics of a servant are prominently displayed in King Jesus.

The characteristics of the servant displayed in Christ

Work to do

Does the servant have work assigned? So did Jesus. He did not come to this earth just 'to get away from it all' for a little while. He did not come here because he was bored with the glories of heaven. He was not in need of a holiday. He came here because a work had been assigned to him, the work of redemption.

The Bible tells us that God the Father, God the Son and God the Holy Spirit, before the world began, agreed with each other on this work of redemption. God knew man would fall into sin, and his heart of grace compelled him to plan a way to redeem man from sin. The centrepiece of this plan was that God the Son, in the fulness of time, would leave the glories of heaven and become a man himself. As a man he was to live in perfect obedience to the law of God, and he was to receive the death penalty that rightfully belonged to guilty sinners. By his life he was to provide the righteousness we do not have and by his death he was to receive the penalty our sins deserved. The child of God, then, is one who has no penalty left to pay because Jesus paid it, and one who can stand faultless before a holy God because he is clothed in the righteousness provided by Christ's perfect life.

This is the great work of redemption and this is what brought the Lord Jesus Christ into this world. And this is why Jesus said he had come to serve and 'to give his life a ransom for many'. He came to do the work he had been assigned.

And just as the servant has no will of his own, so it was with Jesus. In John's Gospel we constantly find Jesus saying he had not come to do his own will, but the will of the Father who sent him (John 4:34; 5:30; 6:38; 12:49-50; 14:10).

Can you imagine a servant deciding to go fishing because

he didn't feel like working? The idea is ludicrous! Servants don't obey at their leisure and according to their pleasure. The master's will is their will. We should be thankful that it was the same with Jesus. He had the servant's mentality, the mentality that bowed to authority, and he refused to depart from the work that had been given him. If it were not for this, we would have no salvation.

Poverty and lowliness

Furthermore, just as the servant is characterized by poverty and lowliness, so was Jesus. He was not born in the capital, Jerusalem, but in tiny Bethlehem (Micah 5:2). He was not born in a palace, but in a stable. He was not surrounded by servants, but by animals. He was not attended by royal physicians, but only by humble parents. He was not greeted by other kings and princes, but only by crude shepherds.

And this lowly beginning was not just an unfortunate episode that was quickly corrected. It was the first instalment of his whole life. From the stable in Bethlehem he went on to the carpenter's shop in Nazareth, and from that humble shop he went into a ministry in which he had nowhere to lay his head.

Suffering

Finally, just as the servant's life is filled with suffering and sorrow, so it was with Jesus. He knew the pain and anguish of rejection. He saw the havoc created by sin, and his sensitive spirit agonized over it. Scripture tells us he wept over the city of Jerusalem (Luke 19:41), and that he was troubled, groaned in his spirit and wept at the tomb of Lazarus (John 11:33,35). It also mentions him sighing (Mark 7:34). The sufferings of his short life finally peaked in the terrible agony of the worst kind of all deaths, the death on the cross.

All of these sufferings fulfilled the prophecy of Isaiah that he would be 'a man of sorrows and acquainted with grief' (Isa. 53:3).

In other words, Jesus' servanthood was not mere pretence. It was not a sham, but real in every aspect. If he came to do the work of a servant, he had to be a servant in every respect.

Did the King of glory stoop so low as to become a servant? What mystery! And did he do this so guilty sinners could be forgiven? What mercy! Charles Wesley captured both the mystery and the mercy of the servant Christ performing the work of redemption:

> 'Tis mystery all! The Immortal dies!
> Who can explain his strange design?
> In vain the first-born seraph tries
> To sound the depths of love divine!
> 'Tis mercy all! Let earth adore,
> Let angel minds enquire no more.

The characteristics of the servant in us

Most of us are quite willing to acknowledge all these truths and even to rejoice in them. But there is another aspect of Jesus' servanthood that makes us shy away — the fact that his followers are also to display the characteristics of the servant.

Jesus' purpose in calling his servanthood to the attention of his disciples was to etch indelibly on their minds the truth that they were to be like him. His words could not be clearer: 'A disciple is not above his teacher, nor a servant above his master' (Matt. 10:24). And Paul's purpose in calling the servanthood of Jesus to the attention of the Philippians was so he could say, 'Let this mind be in you...' (Phil. 2:5).

Work to do

What, then, are the implications of Christ's servanthood for us? It should be quite obvious that if Christ's servanthood meant there was work for him to do, then there must be work for us, his servants, to do. He has provided the work of redemption and there is nothing we can do to add to that, but we do have the responsibility to share the good news of what he has done.

And if Christ's servanthood required him to have no will of his own but to live completely for the Father's will, we who claim to be his servants must learn to submit to his authority.

Poverty and lowliness

Do we dare go to the next step? The servanthood of Jesus caused him to be deprived of the world's goods and live in lowly circumstances. Does this also apply to us? The Bible does indeed command us to live simply and not ostentatiously. It instructs us to avoid making the accumulation of worldly goods our priority, and to support our Lord's work by giving sacrificially from the wealth we have. Jesus himself said we are not to lay up treasures on earth but rather in heaven (Matt. 6:19-21). On another occasion he said, 'Beware of covetousness, for one's life does not consist in the abundance of the things he possesses' (Luke 12:15). And Paul added this word: 'And having food and clothing, with these we shall be content' (1 Tim. 6:8).

Suffering

Finally, just as Jesus' servanthood involved suffering, so will our service to him. He said, 'Remember the word that I said to you, "A servant is not greater than his master." If they persecuted me, they will also persecute you' (John 15:20). Serve the Lord and, sooner or later, you will encounter misunderstanding, ridicule and scorn. It is part and parcel of being his servant.

What is our response to these things? Can we truthfully say we are working for the one who did so much work for us? Do we feel a great debt of gratitude for the whole work of redemption? Do we think in terms of being servants?

Christmas is the best of all times for giving ourselves afresh to service, because servanthood is right at the heart of Christmas. This Christmas let's thank God for sending our Servant-King, Jesus, and let's pledge ourselves to follow in his steps.

26.

This king is a shepherd!

Isaiah 40:9-11; Matthew 2:1-6

Have you ever wondered why the angels announced the birth of Jesus to shepherds? It seems that the birth of the King of kings should have been announced to royalty rather than to ordinary shepherds. Did the angels bungle their assignment? Was there some sort of computer foul-up in heaven? No, there was no mistake. God had the birth of the King of kings announced to shepherds because it was appropriate. Jesus was to be a king, but he was also to be a shepherd.

King and shepherd? It sounds like a glaring contradiction. Consider the shepherd of Bible times. First, his life was one of great hardship. He was constantly exposed to the extremes of heat and cold. He usually subsisted on meagre supplies. At times his life was in danger as he defended his sheep from attacks of wild beasts.

His life was also one of dull routine. Each morning he led the flock from the fold to the pasture by going before them and calling to them. At the pasture, he maintained careful watch over the sheep. If one strayed he sought it out and brought it back. He counted the sheep as they entered the fold to make sure none were missing. Since there was usually no door to the sheepfold, the shepherd himself would serve as the door by positioning himself at the opening of the sheepfold. No sheep could leave and no intruder could enter without the shepherd knowing about it.

That is certainly a far cry from the life of a king. The king knew nothing about extreme hardship and dull routine. He was surrounded by scores of people whose sole purpose was to keep him from facing even minor inconveniences. And when the king got bored there were any number of avenues he could take to find a diversion. The king could travel, throw a party, or call in the court jester.

It seems, in the light of these things, to be utterly ludicrous to mention a king and a shepherd in the same breath, let alone suggest that one person could be both. But this is, in fact, what the passages cited above tell us about Jesus. He is both Shepherd and King, the Shepherd-King. In other words, he is the king who rules in the manner of a shepherd. He combines a king's authority with a shepherd's heart.

Christ's coming

This shepherd's heart is what brought him to this world in the first place. We need to remind ourselves frequently that he did not have to come. Sometimes we forget this. We slip easily into thinking he came because he saw something in us. The truth is that he came, not because of anything in us, but rather because of his own heart of grace. The apostle Paul put it like this: 'For when we were still without strength, in due time Christ died for the ungodly... But God demonstrates his own love toward us, in that while we were still sinners, Christ died for us' (Rom. 5:6,8).

Paul also wrote to the Corinthians: 'For you know the grace of our Lord Jesus Christ, that though he was rich, yet for your sakes he became poor, that you through his poverty might become rich' (2 Cor. 8:9).

Your enjoyment of the Christmas season will increase im- measurably the moment you realize the Lord Jesus didn't have to lift one finger to save us. We were not even worth saving, but he still came. Why did he do it? It was his shepherd's heart. While our Lord was engaged in his earthly ministry he looked upon the multitudes and 'He was moved with compassion for them, because they were weary and scattered, like sheep having no shepherd' (Matt. 9:36).

That could equally well have been said of the Lord Jesus before he ever stepped into this world. He saw us ruined by sin and facing eternal destruction, and he came. It would have been impressive if Jesus had been so moved by our dilemma that he came down to observe it and to participate in it. But here is how great is his shepherd's heart: he came not just to experience our dilemma but to do something about it. He actually went so far as to die on the cross for guilty sinners. This is how we became his sheep. He purchased us with his own precious blood! (1 Peter 1:18-19). As we have already seen, he had a covenant or agreement with God before the world began that he would go to the cross and receive in his own body the penalty our sins so richly deserve. It is through what the author of Hebrews calls 'the blood of the everlasting covenant' (Heb. 13:20-21) that we have our sins forgiven and enjoy peace with God.

Jesus himself said, 'I am the good shepherd. The good shepherd gives his life for the sheep' (John 10:11). Christian, don't let the glitter of our Christmas observances obscure his shepherd's heart that brought him, not just to be with us, but to die for us.

Christ's shepherdly care

It is this same shepherd's heart that causes him to watch over us and care for us. Several things are involved in caring for sheep.

Feeding the sheep

The most obvious task is to make sure they have something to eat. Our Lord's shepherdly care has caused him to provide abundant food for us. What is the food for his sheep? It is the Word of God. Through this Word we grow into full 'sheephood'.

Have you ever stopped to ponder the marvellous provisions your shepherd has made for your spiritual nourishment? Churches, pastors, teachers, books — all have been put in place by the Shepherd for his sheep. The shame is that we have so many scrawny sheep in the midst of such abundance.

Bringing back the straying

Another aspect of the shepherd's care is to bring back those who are straying. Sheep do have a tendency to stray. If you are one of the Lord's sheep, you do not need anyone to tell you this. You know it all too well because you constantly feel it in your heart. Here, straying sheep, is your consolation: your Shepherd will not allow you to stray so far that you are lost for ever. The Lord has never lost a sheep and he never will (John 10:27-30). When you stray he will come after you, find you and restore you to the flock.

The downside of this is that if you stray and the Shepherd never restores you, it is because you were not one of his sheep to begin with (1 John 2:19).

Protecting the sheep

Still another aspect of our Lord's shepherdly care is that he protects us from danger. Yes, sheep have enemies. David, in the process of caring for his sheep, had to kill both bears and

lions (1 Sam. 17:34-37). Our enemies, however, are more ferocious and fearsome than mere bears and lions. We are up
against Satan himself, the lusts of the flesh and the constant
pull of the world. Sometimes we feel our enemies are too great
for us and we begin to lose heart, but the Bible assures us that
our Shepherd has never lost a battle and we may be confident
that he will see us safely home to our heavenly fold. There no
enemy will be able to touch us. Paul tells us the last enemy to
be destroyed will be death itself, all will be brought into complete subjection to Christ and God will be 'all in all' (1 Cor.
15:26-28).

All of this leads me to a final consideration, which is that
the shepherd heart of our Lord causes his sheep to follow him.

Christ's effectiveness as a shepherd

This brings me to the danger of turning the Bible's 'will's into
'should's. We read these passages about the Lord being the
Shepherd of his people and, in the light of them, we say we
'should' follow him. But Jesus said something quite different:
'My sheep hear my voice, and I know them, and they follow
me' (John 10:27).

Those words do not contain any exhortation. Jesus was
making a flat affirmation that his sheep will follow him. Yes,
sheep stray, but temporarily straying is quite different from
not following the shepherd at all. Those who claim to have the
Lord as their shepherd and yet do not have the inclination to
follow him are proclaiming that they really do not know the
Shepherd at all.

What a joy it is to have ruling over us a king who is really a
shepherd at heart! His shepherd's heart caused him to come
and give his life for his sheep. His shepherd's heart causes him

to care for us faithfully and tenderly. Once we see these truths we will find ourselves longing to follow him. No sheep ever had a better shepherd!

I began by talking about how appropriate it was for Jesus' birth to be announced to shepherds. Do you remember what these shepherds did after hearing these marvellous tidings? Luke tells us they went to Bethlehem to see the new king. After they drank in the sight, the Bible tells us they did two things: they made it 'widely known' that he had been born and they returned to their flocks 'glorifying and praising God.' (Luke 2:17,20).

All the Lord's people should celebrate the birth of Jesus in exactly the same way as those men did: telling the good news and praising God for what he has done.

Section VIII

The songs of Christmas

27

The song of Elizabeth

Luke 1:39-45

In the Gospel of Luke we find five songs associated with the birth of Christ: the songs of Elizabeth (1:39-45), Mary (1:46-55), Zacharias (1:67-79), the angels (2:14) and Simeon (2:29-32).

No, they are not songs in the way we normally think of the word. Only one appears to be the type of song that could actually be sung, and that is the song of the angels on the night Jesus was born (2:14). But they are all very definitely metrical compositions. In fact, newer translations print all these songs, with the exception of Elizabeth's, in the form of poetry.

Even though these translations do not set out Elizabeth's song in the form of poetry, William Hendriksen maintains that her words have definite poetic characteristics. He says, 'The parallelistic structure of the lines, so characteristic of Hebrew and Aramaic poetry, the balanced form and neatly arranged clauses ... mark them as being indeed a poem; or, if one prefers, a song, Elizabeth's Song.'[1]

In the last analysis, of course, the form of the words is not all that important. What really counts is their meaning. What was Elizabeth saying here? Why should we be interested in her words?

Elizabeth spoke these words to Mary. Both women were pregnant. Elizabeth was carrying John the Baptist and Mary was carrying Jesus. Both these women were looking forward to the birth of their babies. But they were also looking forward to the birth of Mary's baby in a special way. It was his birth that signalled the beginning of Christmas.

We might say, then, that Mary's visit to Elizabeth and their conversations about the babies they would bear constituted the first celebration of Christmas. Their celebration can help us with our own celebrations.

Are we ready to celebrate Christmas from our hearts? Are we even now rejoicing in the truths it brings before us? Or are we depressed, despondent and in the holiday doldrums?

Elizabeth's song contains the secrets to enjoying Christmas. Put them into practice and Christmas will be a sheer joy and delight. Leave them out and Christmas will find us feeling frustrated and empty. What are these secrets?

Showing concern for others

Two things are absolutely indisputable about Elizabeth and Mary as they prepared themselves for that first Christmas — both women had been immeasurably and enormously blessed, but Mary had been blessed more than Elizabeth.

Both women were to bear special babies. Elizabeth's baby, John the Baptist, was destined to occupy a unique place in God's scheme of things. He was not only to be the fiery preacher who would call Israel away from their sins and back to God, but he was also to announce the coming of the Messiah. He was to be Christ's forerunner.

But even though John was a great man, Jesus was far greater. For one thing, John was a mere man. He was conceived naturally. Jesus, however, was no mere man. He was, and is, the God-man, conceived supernaturally and born of a virgin.

When these babies grew to manhood, John the Baptist freely and frequently acknowledged the superiority of Jesus. When

Jesus presented himself to John for baptism, John hailed him with the words: 'Behold! The Lamb of God who takes away the sin of the world!' (John 1:29). Still later John said of Jesus, 'He must increase, but I must decrease' (John 3:30).

So we should not be surprised to read that when Mary went to visit Elizabeth two remarkable things happened.

First, as soon as Elizabeth heard Mary's greeting, 'The babe leaped in her womb' (v. 41), and Elizabeth broke out into exuberant praise.

What interests me about Elizabeth is that even though she knew Mary had received a greater blessing than she had herself, she didn't resent it, but pronounced a threefold blessing on Mary. She blessed her for the favour she had found, for the fruit she would bear and for the faith she had shown.

Do you want the formula for not only a blessed Christmas but a blessed life? Here it is, courtesy of Elizabeth: don't live for yourself and your own happiness. This flies in the face of everything society tells us. We are constantly urged to seek our own fulfilment, to 'find' ourselves and to build our self-esteem to the maximum. The happiest people are those who live, not for themselves, but for others. That is not just my idea. Jesus himself taught it: 'For whoever desires to save his life will lose it, but whoever loses his life for my sake will find it' (Matt. 16:25).

That brings us to the second part of Elizabeth's formula for celebrating Christmas.

Giving priority to the Lord

In the midst of heaping blessings on Mary, Elizabeth asks, 'But why is this granted to me, that the mother of my Lord should come to me?' (v. 43).

Two little words in Elizabeth's song almost escape notice — 'my Lord'. Elizabeth saw that, while Mary was blessed in bearing Jesus, her own blessing lay in the fact that Mary's child was to be the Messiah, the Lord of all. Mary could call Jesus 'my child', and that was no small blessing; but both Mary and Elizabeth could call him 'my Lord', and that was the greatest blessing of all.

Mary was blessed to bear Christ, but God's blessing is not limited to her. It rests on all those who, like Elizabeth, recognize what the Word of God teaches about Christ and live in accordance with those teachings (Luke 11:27-28).

Elizabeth had her priorities straight. She had settled life's fundamental issue by acknowledging that Jesus was Lord even before he was born. She knew this because the Word of God had prophesied it and the Holy Spirit had certified it within her heart.

We shall never really be able to celebrate Christmas until we come to share Elizabeth's conviction. One reason why Christmas is so frustrating to so many is that they give priority to the wrong things. Priority belongs to Jesus Christ, the Lord of glory, who stepped into human history to provide salvation for all who receive him as Lord and Saviour.

If we will focus on the Christ of Christmas, we shall find a strange awe and a wonderful warmth about Christmas that we did not think possible. How does one focus on Christ? Those who are not Christians must repent of their sins and place their faith and trust in him. All those who have received Christ should do some evaluating and, if necessary, reshuffle some priorities to give Christ the place of pre-eminence. Whatever focusing on Christ requires of us, we must do it without delay. Only then do we truly celebrate Christmas.

1. William Hendriksen, *New Testament Commentary: Luke,* Baker Book House, p.95.

28.

The song of Mary

Luke 1:46-56

The first Christmas carol was 'sung' by Elizabeth, the mother of John the Baptist. As we saw in the previous chapter, when Mary, the mother of Jesus, came to visit her, Elizabeth burst into a song in which she pronounced a threefold blessing upon Mary.

Elizabeth was right, of course, to bless Mary as she did. Mary was indeed privileged to be the one chosen to bear the Messiah (Luke 1:42), and Mary had shown great faith when the angel Gabriel told her she had been selected for this high honour (vv. 38,45).

But such praise can be very dangerous. With such glowing words echoing in the ears, it is very easy to have an exaggerated view of one's own importance. Mary didn't allow any such notions to gain a toehold. She immediately responded to Elizabeth's song with a song of her own, a song in which she turns the spotlight completely away from herself and puts it where it belongs — on God. She begins by saying, 'My soul magnifies the Lord.'

That word 'magnify' (from which the song gets the title 'the Magnificat') ought to drive us to do some soul-searching. It means to enlarge, or to cause an object to be held in higher esteem or respect. Has it ever occurred to you that each of us is magnifying something? We may be doing it consciously or unconsciously, but we are all putting our life's spotlight on something. What are you magnifying? As others observe you, what is the message that comes across to them? What does your life persuade them to esteem and value? What do they see looming so large in your life that it dominates and dwarfs everything else?

Can you say, like Mary, that you are magnifying God? Or would you have to admit that your life is giving a lot of importance to lesser things?

If you are not consciously living to magnify God, you need Mary's song. It consists of two stanzas, each of which is a powerful incentive for magnifying God. The first says God should be magnified because of what he has done and the second because of the promise he has kept.

The great things he has done (vv. 46-53)

Mary puts it like this: 'For he who is mighty has done great things for me, and holy is his name' (v. 49). To say God has done great things is to say, first, that he is merciful — that he cares enough about people to do something for them; and, secondly, that he is mighty — that he is able to do something for them. Some argue, in the light of all the evil around us, that God either wants to stop the evil and cannot, or that he can stop the evil but will not. Mary affirms over and against these options that God is both good and powerful, or merciful and mighty.

Mercy

Mary saw herself as an indisputable testimony to both God's mercy and might. He had shown his mercy by selecting her to be the mother of Jesus. He could have selected a woman from among the rich, famous and powerful. Instead he picked a common, undistinguished Jewish girl, and elevated her to a unique place. Mary testifies to this in these words: 'For he has regarded the lowly state of his maidservant; for behold, henceforth all generations will call me blessed' (v. 48).

Might

God had also demonstrated his might in and through Mary. The conception and birth of Jesus were the result of God's intervening and interrupting the natural course of events. The angel Gabriel left no doubt about that when he announced to Mary: 'The Holy Spirit will come upon you, and the power of the Highest will overshadow you; therefore, also, that Holy One who is to be born will be called the Son of God... For with God nothing will be impossible' (vv. 35,37).

Even though Mary had experienced the mercy and might of God in a most remarkable fashion, she knew these qualities were not limited to her. In all of his dealings, God exhibits these qualities. Take God's mercy for a moment. Mary says it is 'on those who fear him from generation to generation' (v. 50). In every generation those who reverence God can see countless expressions of his abundant mercy. Does this mean those who do not fear God are not blessed? No, it rather means they cannot see his merciful hand at work in their own generation and in past generations. The child of God, on the other hand, has no difficulty in seeing God's mercy on every page of history and in every day of life.

God has also demonstrated his might time after time. Mary viewed history as nothing more than a record of the mighty acts of God. She declares, 'He has shown strength with his arm...' (v. 51). The arm is a common symbol in the Bible for power. Mary was, of course, well versed in the Old Testament, and she could, therefore, have cited several instances of the proud and mighty being brought low, and the lowly and the hungry being exalted and satisfied (vv. 51-53). (An example of God exalting the lowly is Joseph in Genesis 37-41. An example of God frustrating the mighty is Pharaoh in Exodus 5-13). The 'hungry', in this context, seems to refer to spiritual hunger, a craving for God. Jesus himself promised years later that those who hunger in this way 'shall be filled' (Matt. 5:6). Each instance of the mighty being frustrated and the lowly being elevated Mary viewed as a movement of God's powerful arm.

Perhaps some are tempted to respond to this part of Mary's song by pointing out cases in which the proud did prevail and the lowly were not elevated. I have two observations about such situations. First, where evil has been defeated, God is the one who did it; and, secondly, he has not finished yet. The evil that has continued to exist will not escape his judgement in eternity. There our mighty God will completely triumph over every last vestige of evil.

So the first stanza of Mary's song shows us that God should be magnified because of the great things he had done, things that clearly demonstrated his mercy and might. Now we turn to the second reason why he should be magnified.

The promise he has kept (vv. 54-55)

I realize this does not mean much to our generation. We appear to place little value on a person's keeping his word. Or maybe it would be better to say we expect others to keep their word to us, but we feel no obligation to keep our word to others.

But before you dismiss this matter of God keeping his word as a totally insignificant and irrelevant thing, think for a moment about the promise God kept that first Christmas. Hundreds of years before Mary was born, God had promised he would bless all the families of the earth through Abraham and his descendants. In short, God was promising that one of Abraham's descendants would be the Saviour for the world.

As the years passed God sent prophets to remind the people of this promised Saviour. It is not too much to say the entire Old Testament looks forward to his coming. We can well imagine that, as year after year dragged by, some wavered in their faith and wondered if the promise would ever be fulfilled. Maybe it was all a pipedream, a hoax, a delusion.

Then one day God sent Gabriel to announce to Mary that she had been chosen to be the mother of this promised one: 'And behold, you will conceive in your womb and bring forth a Son, and shall call his name Jesus. He will be great, and will be called the Son of the Highest; and the Lord God will give him the throne of his father David. And he will reign over the house of Jacob for ever, and of his kingdom there will be no end' (vv. 31-34).

When Jesus was ready to embark upon his ministry, John the Baptist publicly heralded him as the promised Saviour saying, 'Behold! The Lamb of God who takes away the sin of the world!' (John 1:29). Still later, after Jesus' death, Paul reflected on this matter of God keeping his promise by sending Jesus and wrote, 'But when the fulness of the time had come, God sent forth his Son, born of a woman, born under the law, to redeem those who were under the law, that we might receive the adoption as sons' (Gal. 4:4-5).

Scripture speaks with one voice. God has kept his promise to send a Saviour by sending his Son Jesus Christ into the world. That in and of itself may not seem terribly important to you, but I assure you it was absolutely vital for God to do this. If he had not kept his promise there would have been no Saviour available to us, and the fact is that we all need a Saviour.

Why do we need a Saviour? The Scriptures tell us it is because we are all sinners. And what is so bad about being a sinner? Most people will readily admit they are sinners, but they cannot see what is so serious about it. As far as they are concerned, sin is a minor problem that can easily be taken care of by just ignoring it, or feebly resolving to do better in the future. But here is where the rub comes in — God cannot ignore sin. He is holy and if he ignored sin, he would be denying and compromising his own nature, and he cannot do that.

Something has to be done about our sins before we can ever have fellowship with God. Are you ready now for some good news? Here it is: God himself has provided the way for our sins to be forgiven, and that way is his Son, Jesus Christ, dying on the cross. On that cross he received the penalty due to us so we could be freed from God's wrath. We receive the saving benefits of Christ's work when the Holy Spirit enlightens us as to our sinful condition and enables us to repent of our sins and trust Christ.

We have a God who has done great things, a God who can be trusted to fulfil his promises. Do you see now why Mary felt like magnifying him? Should we not be doing the same?

29

The song of Zacharias

Luke 1:67-79

The third of the Christmas 'songs' in Luke's Gospel comes from Zacharias. What a dramatic change this man experienced! He was a priest, righteous in the sight of God, walking blamelessly in all the commandments and requirements of the Lord (Luke 1:5-6). But when the angel Gabriel appeared to him with the news that he and his aged, barren wife would be the parents of a son, he refused to believe. That unbelief was very costly. It cost Zacharias his ability to speak. Only after the promise was fulfilled and his son was born did his speech return (vv. 7-22).

What we have in this song, then, is the torrent of praise Zacharias poured out when his speech was restored. These words indicate that he had learned his lesson well. No trace of unbelief is found here. These words are brimming with faith and hope. Zacharias' experience should cause each of us to think long and hard about the cost of refusing to believe God. Nothing is more insulting to God than our refusal to take him at his word.

If you, like Zacharias, had been rendered speechless, and you suddenly found your speech restored, what would you start talking about? Surprisingly enough, Zacharias didn't begin talking about himself and what he had been through. Instead he focused on God. Notice also that he focused on one particular point about God, namely, the salvation he was about to provide through the Messiah who was soon to be born. Salvation is the grand theme of the Bible, and the greatest flights of praise are reserved for it. Part of the shame of the church today is that she is so little occupied with this theme of salvation. The church is at her best when she makes much of the salvation God has provided.

Zacharias' song makes it clear that salvation comes through a person, the long-awaited Messiah of God, Jesus. It contains two names for Christ, names that admirably summarize his work.

The horn of salvation

First, Zacharias calls Christ 'a horn of salvation' (v. 69). What did he mean by this? Several things come to mind when we hear the word 'horn'. We might, for instance, think of the trumpet, and understand Zacharias to say that Christ would proclaim, or herald, salvation. While there is truth in that, it was not what Zacharias had in mind. Or we might think of the 'horn of plenty', and understand Zacharias to say that Christ would provide salvation in abundance. This is also true, but it too fails to come to grips with what Zacharias was saying. He was, of course, steeped in the Old Testament, and we may be sure, therefore, that when he used the word 'horn' it was in the Old Testament sense.

In the Old Testament the word is used in connection with certain animals — the ram, the wild ox, or the bull. Each of these powerful animals used its horns to defeat rivals. The horn, then, symbolizes power and especially destructive power (1 Kings 22:11; Dan. 8:5-7; Zech. 1:18-21). So by calling the coming Christ 'a horn of salvation' Zacharias was saying he, the Christ, would wield destructive power with regard to salvation.

I dare say most of us are not accustomed to thinking of salvation in terms of destructive power being exercised. Why is destructive power needed in this work of salvation? The answer is that there are numerous, powerful enemies of our souls who are totally, fanatically dedicated to preventing our salvation. Our only hope, therefore, lies in someone being powerful enough to defeat these enemies and deliver us from them.

The tragedy of our age is that most people are utterly oblivious to these enemies of their souls. They greet such talk with a quizzical look, a bemused smile and a shrug of their shoulders. Somehow it all sounds just too unreal. Don't be deceived! These enemies are real enough, and sticking our heads in the sand will not make them go away.

Who are these enemies? They are Satan and all his hosts (Eph. 6:11-12), the world and all its temptations (James 4:4; 1 John 2:15-17), the flesh and all its lusts (James 1:14-15) and death itself (1 Cor. 15:26). These are the enemies of the soul, and they do indeed 'hate us' (Luke 1:71).

Are you ready for some good news? Jesus Christ has the power to destroy these enemies and that is exactly what he came to do. The Bible says he has already dealt the fatal blow to Satan (John 16:11; Col. 2:13-15; Heb. 2:14-15; 1 John 3:8), the world (John 16:33) and the flesh (Rom. 8:1-4), and some glorious day that last enemy, death, will be brought under his feet (1 Cor. 15:25-28). True, all these enemies still exist and are still operating but Christ, through the exercise of his power, has ensured their ultimate defeat.

How did Christ go about defeating these enemies? Where did he exert the power to accomplish such a feat? The answer seems utterly ludicrous. He did it by dying on the cross. This sophisticated age is prone to regard such a notion as merely an ancient superstition that a few ignoramuses have managed to keep alive. Few people realize that this idea of power in a crucified Saviour met with no more acceptance then than it does now. Paul said, 'We preach Christ crucified, to the Jews a stumbling block and to the Greeks [Gentiles] foolishness...' But Paul didn't stop there. He went on to say, '... but to those who are called, both Jews and Greeks, Christ the power of God and the wisdom of God' (1 Cor. 1:23-24).

Richard Lenski summarizes it so well: 'For it is surely a foolish and a weak thing to let God's own Son die miserably on the cross... And yet this foolish and this weak thing outranks and absolutely outdoes all the wisdom and power of men... If men were asked how God should proceed to save the world they would certainly not say by sending his Son to the cross. Yet this is what God did, and, behold this act saves! So wise is this foolish thing, so powerful this weak thing.'[1]

Christ, then, is the 'horn of salvation' because he came to exercise destructive power against the enemies of our souls.

The Dayspring from on high

That brings us to consider the second name Zacharias uses for Jesus, 'the Dayspring from on high' (Luke 1:78).

The word 'dayspring' means 'sunrise' or 'dawn'. Zacharias was asserting, therefore, that the coming of the Messiah would dispel the darkness and inaugurate a new day. But what does the darkness represent?

Scripture uses the word to convey three things: delusion, depravity and despondency.

Regarding darkness as delusion, Paul tells us that the god of this world has blinded the minds of the unbelieving, that they might not see the light of the gospel of the glory of Christ (2 Cor. 4:4).

Regarding darkness as depravity, Paul warns us to 'walk as children of light', and not to participate in the 'unfruitful works of darkness'. He goes on to explain by saying, 'It is shameful even to speak of those things which are done by them in secret' (Eph. 5:8-12).

Regarding darkness as despondency, the prophet Isaiah pictures his people as being in a state of 'gloom' and 'anguish'. And this was all due to the fact that they were walking 'in darkness' (Isa. 8:22).

There certainly is no shortage of darkness today. People are so deluded that they cannot see the truth and, consequently, they live in depravity and despondency. The people of darkness often try to give the impression of being unusually enlightened, liberated and happy, but all this is no more than a brave front to hide the desperation and emptiness they feel.

There is hope for deluded, depraved, despondent people. Where is this hope to be found? It is all right there in the Christmas message. Jesus Christ is the light that drives the darkness of sin and sorrow away. Through him delusion is dispelled because he grants true knowledge of God. Paul says we see 'the light of the knowledge of the glory of God in the face of Jesus Christ' (2 Cor. 4:6). Through Christ the depravity of sin is dealt with because he gives power for us to live righteously. Paul says to Christians, 'Now you are light in the Lord. Walk as children of light' (Eph. 5:8). Through Christ despondency is destroyed. Those who know him find true peace and joy. In the words of the prophet Malachi, they 'skip about like calves released from the stall' (Mal. 4:2, NASB). The prophet Isaiah says when people who walk in darkness see the light, 'They rejoice before you' (Isa. 9:3).

But if Christ is the dawning of a new day, why is there still so much darkness around? Why is the whole world not bathed in light? The answer is that Christ is the dawn only in the hearts of those who believe in him. The Bible says, 'But as many as received him, to them he gave the right to become children of God, to those who believe in his name...' (John 1:12). As long as men and women continue to love darkness, darkness will prevail. It is only when they turn from darkness and embrace Christ's light that the darkness flees away.

So if you want to be delivered from the enemies of your soul, and if you want the darkness of delusion, depravity and despondency to be dispelled, turn to Christ in repentance and faith. He is the horn of salvation and the Dayspring from on high.

1. R. C. H. Lenski, *The Interpretation of St Paul's First and Second Epistles to the Corinthians,* Augsburg Publishing House, p.71.

30.
The song of the angels

Luke 2:8-20

We live in a day of renegotiation. It is not at all unusual to read about a professional athlete wanting to renegotiate his contract. It doesn't seem to matter if he recently signed a long-term, lucrative contract. He sees some of his peers getting even better contracts and he concludes he is entitled to do the same. So he begins to sulk, threaten and throw assorted temper tantrums until his employer caves in and gives him the new contract he wants.

This renegotiating mentality has crept into the arena of God's dealings with man. Perhaps it is never more evident than at the Christmas season. You don't have to be unusually shrewd to see that there is a concerted and massive effort to renegotiate Christmas. Specifically, our society evidences an intense desire to remove all religious content from Christmas.

Just take a quick look at current Christmas celebrations. Don't you get the distinct impression that Christmas has no objective meaning at all, that it is a nose of wax that can be twisted and shaped to suit one's own personal whims? Some people twist the nose and say Christmas means family togetherness. Others walk up, give the nose a twist, and say Christmas means the spirit of giving and sharing. Still others stroll up, take hold of the nose of wax, twist it and come away saying Christmas is all about peace on earth and goodwill towards men.

The more Christmas gets twisted and distorted, the more we need the fourth of the Christmas songs, the song of the angels. This song clearly reveals that Christmas is not a matter of mere personal preference and whim. It declares that God has defined Christmas once and for all and the matter is not open for discussion, debate and negotiation.

To appreciate the full import of the song we need to look at three things: the announcement that precipitated it (Luke 2:8-13), the song itself (v. 14) and the response of the shepherds to it (vv. 15-20).

Luke tells us that a whole host of angels joined in singing the song recorded in verse 14. But the singing of this angelic host was preceded by the announcement of a single angel.

The announcement

An assurance

This announcement consisted of three parts. First, the angel gave the shepherds a word of assurance. It is easy to see why they needed this. There they were, in the midst of what seemed to be nothing more than just another ordinary, boring night in the life of a shepherd. Suddenly this angel appeared with the glory of God himself shining all around him! This is not the type of thing that makes one yawn and throw another log on the fire! This sight terrified them! So the angel first allayed their fears by telling them he had come to bring 'good tidings of great joy' (v. 11).

The core of the announcement

He then proceeded to the core of his announcement: 'For there is born to you this day in the city of David a Saviour, who is Christ the Lord' (v. 11).

Have you ever stopped to ponder the three titles the angel used for Jesus? First, he is 'Saviour'. That means he is the deliverer of his people. Most of the Jews automatically equated deliverance with liberation from the bondage of Rome, but the Bible is quite clear that Jesus came to deliver his people, the people chosen by his Father (Eph. 1:4) and given to him (John 6:37,39; 17:2,6,9,24), from their sins (Matt. 1:21).

The word 'Christ' means 'Anointed One'. It is an official title designating Jesus as the promised Messiah. In the Old Testament, the word 'anointed' is applied to three distinct offices. Priests were anointed with holy oil (Lev. 4:3-5,16). Prophets were called 'the anointed of God' (Ps. 105:15). And the King of Israel was called on various occasions 'the anointed of the Lord' (1 Sam. 2:10,35).

Study the life and ministry of Jesus and you will find that his work encompassed each of these offices. In his preaching, he performed the work of the prophet, representing God to men. In his death on the cross, he performed the work of the priest, representing men to God. And he is even now at the right hand of the Father, from where he rules and reigns over all those who believe.

The word 'Lord' means 'Master' or 'Exalted One'. Yes, Jesus has been designated and anointed by the Father to be King. But we need to realize that he is Lord over all by virtue of his own person. He is God himself and, therefore, has authority over all. He has always been Lord. He was Lord before there was ever a plan of redemption and before he was ever designated as the Messiah.

A sign

So a special baby had been born. But there must have been many babies in Bethlehem that night. How were the shepherds to know which baby was the one spoken of by the angel? The final part of the angel's announcement consists of a sign: 'You

will find a babe wrapped in swaddling clothes, lying in a manger' (v. 12). Out of all the babies in Bethlehem that night, only
one would be found in a lowly stable, lying in a manger! Oh,
how low the God of heaven stooped to provide redemption
— all the way from heaven's glory to a stable!

Take these three parts of the angel's announcement and
look at them. What can they mean except that there is a very
definite and distinct content to the Christmas message? The
angel did not say, 'Something marvellous has happened, but
just what it is and where it happened is unclear. Try, therefore,
to figure it out for yourselves, and that's what Christmas will
mean to you.' No, the angel was specific and definite! A Saviour had been born! The Christ had been born! The Lord had
been born! And this was not some kind of vague, ambiguous
spiritual experience. He was a real baby and could be found
that very moment in Bethlehem!

An anthem of praise

It was this announcement that caused a whole host of angels
to burst into this song of adoring praise: 'Glory to God in the
highest, and on earth peace, goodwill toward men!'

Most people are quite ready and willing to embrace the last
half of this song. Nothing lights their fire or rings their chimes
like the thought of peace on this weary, war-torn earth. Just
the mere mention of peace and goodwill makes them all teary-
eyed and emotional. When the time comes to purchase their
Christmas cards they invariably select those that use this phrase.
And this is the part of the Christmas carols they always sing
most lustily. But start talking to them about the first part of
this angelic strain and they begin to get nervous and fidgety.
They like the peace and the goodwill, but they don't want to
bow before God and say, 'Glory to God in the highest!'

The great irony is that for all the emphasis we place on peace and goodwill there is precious little of it in this dark world. Talk to those who embrace this part of the Christmas message about why peace and goodwill are so scarce and they will go down their well-worn, familiar paths. They will talk about the need for better education, better environment and better government.

But the Bible maintains that man's basic problem is that he is a sinner. As such he is not capable of permanently producing peace and goodwill until his heart is changed. He needs deliverance from his sinful nature. In other words, he needs the Saviour the angel announced. Thank God, the angel had an announcement to make! The Saviour man needs has come! He came in the form of that tiny baby in Bethlehem.

Only if we see the depth of our sins and our helplessness to do anything about our condition will we truly be able to appreciate Christmas. But once we see our true condition, we will never be willing to settle for only the second half of the Christmas message. We will, like the angels, sing, 'Glory to God in the highest…'

Christmas means God has done something. It means he has sent the Saviour. And if we are to have peace on earth and goodwill towards men, we must have the Saviour. The great tragedy of our day is that people want what the Saviour can provide without embracing the Saviour himself. But the two cannot be separated. It has often been pointed out that we cannot have peace without the Prince of Peace.

The response of the shepherds

We must not leave the song of the angels without considering the shepherds' response. Try to picture yourself being with those shepherds that night. Suppose you had heard the one angel announce the birth of Jesus and all the other angels burst into praise. What would you have done? You certainly would not have fluffed up your pillow and gone to sleep! Surely, you would have done the same thing those shepherds did: they went to see the baby (vv. 15-16), they shared the good news of Jesus with all they met (vv. 17-18) and they praised and glorified God for all they had seen and heard (v. 20).

Don't you think we ought to be doing the same even now? Although we were not there that night to hear the song of the angels, it has come down through the years of time to sound again. You must do, then, as the shepherds did. Seek the Saviour. Don't rest until you have found him and made him your Lord and Saviour. And then tell others about the Saviour you have found. And don't forget to praise the God of heaven for sending such a Saviour to this sinful world.

The meaning of Christmas is settled. It isn't our place to debate and dispute it but, by God's grace, to receive and rejoice in it.

31

The song of Simeon

Luke 2:25-35

Many people go through a vicious cycle every year at this time. They spend weeks and weeks getting hyped up for Christmas only to find it just does not live up to their expectations. Their disappointment may be due to something as childish as not being pleased with the gifts they received. Or it may be something as serious as feeling the full weight of financial difficulties. It may be due to the thought of settling back into the humdrum monotony of daily living. Whatever the reason, many find even before Christmas Day is over that the dark cloud of 'post-holiday blues' has been pulled over the bright sunshine of anticipation and excitement.

The fifth and final of Luke's Christmas songs can help all such people. It brings before us Simeon, a man who was not at all disappointed with Christmas. He waited a long time for the first Christmas to come and when it finally arrived he was entirely and completely satisfied with it. We might, then, call Simeon's song 'the song of satisfaction'.

Are you singing that song these days? The truth is that satisfaction is a very rare and slippery commodity these days. We spend most of our lives looking for it. We look for it in our careers, our families and our possessions, but it always seems to elude us. We rush out to buy the latest best seller on how to find it, but the sure-fire formula we find there fails to kindle so much as one spark of satisfaction in us. We decide to invest our time and money in going to seminars, counselling sessions and self-help groups, only to find ourselves a little poorer and a little more disillusioned. No matter where we look or what we try, it seems satisfaction and fulfilment are just around the next corner or just over the next hill. Millions in our society have no will to go around another corner or up another hill. Filled with despair, they have turned to drugs, alcoholic beverages, gambling, or any one of the other common addictions of our day.

If we are ever to sing Simeon's song of satisfaction, we have to understand that the song of satisfaction requires two things — the right singer and the right subject.

The singer

I get the impression from what Luke says that Simeon was a satisfied man. Satisfaction wasn't something he felt for just the fleeting moments described in this passage. The satisfaction of those moments sprang largely from the type of man Simeon was.

Luke uses four terms to describe Simeon. First, he was 'just'; that is, his conduct was beyond reproach. Then he was 'devout'. This word comes from the Greek word *'eulabes'* which means 'taking hold well'. Simeon was one who had taken hold of God. He reverenced God and was cautious about doing anything to offend God. In addition to that, Luke says Simeon was 'waiting for the Consolation of Israel'. In a day when the Messianic hope had grown dim, Simeon clung tenaciously to it. Finally, Luke says, 'The Holy Spirit was upon him.' That means his thoughts, his words and his deeds gave evidence of one who was controlled by God.

Because Simeon was this type of man, Luke says he received a special revelation from God that he would not die until he had seen the promised Messiah. God always delights in pouring extraordinary blessings upon those who live closest to him. Those who make it their business to know God in a special way are granted special insights into God and his Word.

All of this makes me wonder if many of us are not beginning at the wrong end in this business of finding satisfaction in life. We keep telling ourselves that our lack of satisfaction is all due to the failures of others and to circumstances beyond our control. If we could just get others to toe the mark and if we could get our circumstances whipped into shape, all would be well. Simeon arises from the pages of Scripture to tell us satisfaction is not something that happens instantaneously when all our circumstances are right and when all our stars are in a certain configuration. Instead it is the by-product of living a righteous, dedicated life that clings to the promises of God.

Don't think for a moment that you will ever be able to sing Simeon's song until you live Simeon's life. But how are we to go about living like Simeon did? This kind of life is not produced by sheer will-power. It requires a higher power, the power of God himself to be at work in us. And God works in us to produce this kind of life when our sins are forgiven and we are restored to fellowship with him.

The subject

In other words, no one can be the right kind of singer for the song of satisfaction until he realizes what the subject of that song is. Are you ready for a surprise? The subject of the song of satisfaction is not satisfaction. That is what most of us think it is, but it is not. The theme of the song of satisfaction is salvation. As long as we insist on seeking satisfaction, we shall never find it. When we seek salvation, satisfaction will find us!

Just look at Simeon's song. Yes, it is the song of a satisfied man, but it is about the salvation Jesus had come to provide.

What is this salvation Simeon sang about? What kind of salvation did Jesus come to provide? There were many people in Simeon's day who believed the Messiah would provide salvation of a temporal sort. They looked for him to throw off the cruel Roman oppression they were chafing under and to usher in a golden age. To their way of thinking, this kingdom would be one in which the Jewish nation would be exalted to a position of supremacy and all the Gentile powers and peoples would be crushed and suppressed.

But those who held these notions had misread their Old Testament. The common theme of the Old Testament is that the Messiah would come to deliver people from a tyrannical power far greater than the hated Romans — that is, the power of sin. And the kingdom the Messiah would set up would not be temporal in nature, but spiritual, one in which he would rule and reign in the hearts of all who would receive him. Furthermore, his kingdom would not be for Jews only but also for Gentiles (v. 32).

While most of his generation somehow missed all this, Simeon saw it clearly. You see, if Simeon had thought of the Messiah's work in the same terms as most of the Jews, he would never had said to Mary what he did. Look at these sombre words: 'Behold, this child is destined for the fall and rising of many in Israel, and for a sign which will be spoken against (yes, a sword will pierce through your own soul also), that the thoughts of many hearts may be revealed' (v. 34).

If Jesus had been the kind of Messiah most of the Jews were looking for, Simeon's words would have been meaningless. Jesus would have been hailed and followed, not spoken against and opposed. But because he came to deal with sin, he was destined to encounter hostility and hatred of the first order. There is nothing sinful man hates more than having his wicked nature called to his attention. Nothing arouses his anger more than being told he stands guilty before a holy God and he must repent. But this is the message Jesus came to preach, and in doing it he stirred up so much hatred and resentment that they crucified him. That crucifixion was, of course, the sword that pierced Mary's heart.

Knowing what Simeon knew about the salvation Jesus came to provide, can you imagine how he must have felt when he took the baby Jesus into his arms? That baby was Simeon's Saviour! That baby was Simeon's deliverer from the bondage of sin and from eternal condemnation. That baby was Simeon's passage to eternal glory! It would be a great thrill to hold a baby destined for some kind of greatness. How indescribably thrilling it must be to hold in your very own arms the Son of God himself, the one who had come to pay for all your sins so you could stand clean before a holy God and inherit heaven as your eternal home!

Are you interested in this grand theme of salvation? You should be! You will never find peace and satisfaction in this life until you make salvation your primary concern. There is a God-shaped vacuum in us that can only be filled by God. Saint Augustine wrote, 'Thou madest us for thyself, and our heart is restless, until it repose in thee.'[1]

The sad truth is that many want the satisfaction Simeon had without prizing the salvation he prized. But the two are welded inseparably together and cannot be disconnected. If you want satisfaction, embrace Simeon's Saviour and Lord, Jesus Christ. The song of satisfaction springs only from those who do.

---

1. *The Confessions of St Augustine,* Zondervan Publishing House, p.7.